W9-AQW-857

The Write Treatment Anthology
Volume I 2011-2016

GLEN COVE, NEW YORK 11542-...
4 GLEN COVE AVENUE
GLEN COVE PUBLIC LIBRARY

The Write Treatment Anthology
Volume I 2011-2016

WRITINGS BY CANCER PATIENTS,
SURVIVORS, AND CAREGIVERS
FROM THE WRITE TREATMENT
WORKSHOPS AT MOUNT SINAI
WEST AND MOUNT SINAI BETH
ISRAEL CANCER CENTERS, NYC

Emily Rubin, Editor/Instructor
Lauren Flick, Editor
Laura Rader, Illustrations

This anthology is a compilation of fiction, memoir and poetry. Some names and characteristics have been changed to protect the privacy of individuals. Any opinions and experiences described regarding individuals or institutions are those of the authors and do not reflect the views of the editors or of Mount Sinai.

Copyright © 2016 Emily Rubin
All rights reserved.

ISBN: 0692776184
ISBN 13: 9780692776186

The Write Treatment Anthology Volume I: 2011–2016

Writings by Cancer Patients, Survivors, and Caregivers from
The Write Treatment Workshops
Mount Sinai West and Mount Sinai Beth Israel, NYC

Table of Contents

Preface

Dear Reader,

Welcome to *The Write Treatment Anthology Volume I.* This book is a collection of literature written by cancer patients, survivors, and caregivers who have participated in The Write Treatment Creative Writing Workshops at Mount Sinai Hospitals in New York City.

At each weekly workshop, with writing prompts, photographs, and inspirational quotes, we write together. The participants are welcome to explore the experience of diagnosis and treatment, which they do, but many use the time to take a much-needed furlough from cancer, and in each case the imagination takes flight. With eyes squinting, brows furrowed, and pervasive sighs, they begin to glide their pens across blank pages. It is thrilling to see the imaginings percolate so quickly. Eager and impatient to share, we read back from the penned pages that span the literary landscape.

I was diagnosed with breast cancer in 2008 and underwent treatment until 2010 at Mount Sinai Beth Israel. A year after finishing treatment I was thrilled to find out that my novel, *Stalina*, was a winner of the Amazon Debut Novel Award Contest. The award included a publishing contract. My cancer diagnosis was life changing, but so was becoming a published author. Soon after receiving the wonderful news about my novel, I found signs of a possible relapse of the cancer. Fortunately, tests came back negative. The angst I experienced was an acknowledgment that cancer would always be part of my psyche, if not my body. I wanted to find a constructive way to face these anxieties. I wanted to find a way to give back to the community of patients, doctors and nurses, friends, colleagues, and family who supported me throughout my cancer journey.

With the exception of sparse, mostly one-line entries in a journal, I put my writing practice on hold during treatment. The rigors of surgery, chemo, radiation, insurance companies, and mounting bills were overwhelming. So the manuscript for the novel sat in a drawer untouched for more than a year. I felt guilty about not writing, but I did not want to burden a group or workshop with all my medical drama, and I didn't want my entire identity to be about cancer. At the time it didn't occur to me that a place to write could be a haven from treatment. The hospital had programs for patients, such as knitting, Reiki, and yoga, but no writing workshops in the offerings. With my writing life back on track after the publication of my novel, I thought a workshop could be a viable way for people affected by cancer to process, think, and write about their experiences.

Five years ago I approached the social-work team at Mount Sinai Beth Israel Hospital with the idea of running creative writing workshops for cancer patients, survivors, and caregivers.

"Great idea. Go for it!" the social-work team said.

Five years later the workshops have become an integral part of Mount Sinai's services. Last year more than three hundred participants attended the sixty plus workshops. *The Write Treatment Anthology Volume I* is a tribute to their dedication.

The twenty writers included in the anthology have shown a fierce commitment to the process, showing up during trying times in treatment, and even during New York City blizzards. They have been fearless in acknowledging and addressing their experiences and the unknown—reflecting on Grace Paley's words, "We write about what you don't know about what you know." Their enthusiasm is here in the array of subjects and down-to-the-bone honesty throughout the stories and poems you will encounter.

Taking chances, making hard choices, being fierce and vulnerable, and embracing humor are all part of life with cancer, and, as we have discovered in the workshops, essential to writing. I have seen The Write Treatment Workshops grow from a gathering of people affected by cancer into a community of dedicated writers.

Whether memoir, fiction, or poetry, risk-taking is evident in the fierce, funny, touching, and sometimes risqué musings around the table. That the writing is artful and cathartic is not surprising. Laughter, tears, and prickling energy fill the room, and after two hours we part feeling enervated and inspired. This is the magic, joy, and solace of writing in a group. The writers in this anthology are as diverse as passengers on any NYC subway or bus—these are the voices of a community filled with empathy and words unencumbered. These stories and poems are written by a group willing to experiment and explore in times of trouble the worlds within and without.

I would like to thank Dennis Paoli of the Heidi Paoli Fund, whose support for the workshops and anthology made this book possible. I am grateful to the dedicated and energetic social-work staff of Mount Sinai Beth Israel and Mount Sinai West: Alison Snow, Lori Schwartz, Nancy Borque, and Sandy Lansinger, for their enthusiasm and continued administrative and moral support for the workshops.

A side note: My dear friends Robert Lee and Kathrin Marx, with the help of many others, organized a benefit to raise money to cover the expenses for my cancer treatment. To Kathrin, Robert, the artists, and the businesses that donated auction items, a restaurant, food and drink (Phil Hartman of Two Boots Pizzeria rocks!), and to those who bid on every item, I am forever indebted. My community supported me through a difficult time, and this was the most natural thing in the world for all those involved. The generosity and work continue. Thank you for your support in reading and spreading the word about our book and the workshops.

Emily Rubin, author/instructor, September 2016

We see the brightness of a new page where
anything yet can happen.

-RAINER MARIA RILKE

In memory of
our colleague and teacher Susan Ribner
and
artist and writer Caroline M. Sun.
Great friends, brilliant minds.

Susan Ribner

EDITOR'S NOTE: *THE FIRST CHAPTER of this anthology is devoted to the writings of my colleague Susan Ribner, who passed away in October 2014 after a four-and-a-half year battle with cancer. Susan and I were running separate writing workshops in Mount Sinai hospitals. Bonnie Marcus, the director of the Poets and Writers East Coast Readings and Workshops Program, which provided funding for the workshops, encouraged us to talk about the work. Sue and I had many conversations and organized several readings for the participants to share the work with family and friends. We had different approaches to the workshops. My workshops were fiction and poetry infused, while Susan was devoted to*

memoir. *We both agreed the workshops were magical. While Sue was in hospice at home, she asked if I would take over her workshop at Mount Sinai West (formerly Roosevelt). It was with a heavy heart and a sense of pride for the work that I agreed to continue in her place. Her dedication to the process lives on in the workshops.*

FRONT LAWN/BACKYARD STORIES

The following selections were published in *Quarterly West*, Fall 2011 (Issue 72)—a winner of the issue's Nonfiction Award.

I WRITE A BOOK
1945

The screen door swings open, and I appear, clutching a load of objects in my small arms. I stand for a few seconds at the top of the cement steps, squinting in the summer sun. A sweet breeze twists the pinafore around my skinny legs. Across Liberty Street, my sister and Sally O'Hara are running circles around Sally's house, yelling for some reason.

I am going to write a book.

Onto the newly mown grass I waddle under my heavy cargo and then set out my goods, more seriously than at a tea party: the slips of white paper I've taken off my father's desk; the thick red book pulled at random from my mother's bookcase; and my cherished fifth birthday present—my toy typewriter. My palms glide over its shiny surface, my fingers tracing the brightly colored circle of alphabet letters.

I know how to work it. I've practiced twisting the center dial until the arrow points to a letter. Then I press hard on the dial, and the typewriter clunks and prints on the paper.

I will copy and type every word in this grown-up book.

Robins bounce around the yard. Blue jays racket in the trees. Margo and Sally have yelped across to this side of the street and now leap-frog back and forth over the fire hydrant on the other side of the hedge.

I am copying, letter by letter, twisting the miracle dial, hitting the clunker with my small fists.

Margo's voice booms into the yard. "What are you doing, Susie?" She peeks over the hedge, her cat-like eyes tilting upward, crinkling in her devil way.

"I'm busy," I say, hoping she leaves. "Writing a book."

"That's ridiculous, Susie!" Margo says, snorting pig noises through her nose as she and Sally run off down Liberty Street.

I won't listen to her. I type and I type, and the *book* appears on my paper, the letters crooked and smudged. It doesn't look good, but I keep typing.

Time goes on forever. The sun drops behind the trees, and I sit in shadows. My wrists hurt. The mosquitoes bite my legs and arms. And my tired eyes scan the messy letters in their long, uneven lines—all *two* of them.

Slowly, slowly, I take in my folly—the huge gap between my grand scheme and my small ability. My chest and head fill with a blunt, gray sense of failure. I understand. I will never be able to write a book.

My mother appears on the front steps, wiping her hands on her apron. She whistles for Margo and me the familiar "Daddy will be home soon, so come get ready for dinner" tune.

I scrape the grass off my legs; scratch my bites; then gather up my machine, the book, and the sad papers; and carry it all across the grass.

"What have you been doing?" my mother asks, chipper.

I want to tell her that I tried to write a book and couldn't. And now I want to cry. But I sense she doesn't want bad news. "Oh, nothing," I say.

CONFUCIUS AND THE CHERRY TREE
1946

Up in the backyard cherry tree, Margo and I straddle branches, her perch higher than mine, as we collect plump cherries for Mommy in brown paper bags. It's a small tree, easy enough for us to climb and secluded from the front yard by the trellis and the tall white fence.

We eat one cherry for each that we save—so juicy and deep-red like the roses Daddy tends on the trellis, like the rose Margo will wear in her hair when she later becomes a gypsy dancer. We spit the pits into the yard, competing to blow them the farthest, and while we do, Margo teaches me my first off-color jokes. She uses bad words, more nastier than "doo-doo," the worst in my vocabulary so far. There's no one around but the robins.

Today, it's a song to "Smoke Gets in Your Eyes." Margo swings her legs back and forth and sings: *They asked me how I knew /Chipmunk shit was blue / I just smiled and said / You have been misled /Chipmunk shit is red.*

A thrill goes through me, or is it a shiver, as I hear the bad word? But I like Margo's daring, her badness. We laugh and laugh until our stomachs hurt and we wet our pants.

"Wait 'til you hear this one, Susie!" Her mouth full of cherries, Margo recites: "Confucius say, 'Woman who fly plane upside down soon have crack up!'"

I need this joke explained. When I get it, I marvel at its clever double meaning, its raciness.

A few weeks later, my mother's parents, the Lewins, visit from Boston. I know Grandpa loves jokes, but still I'm nervous as I approach him in the den where he rests on the sleep-away bed. Here he is this late afternoon, his large body slumped on the Mexican spread, his eyes closed, the *Wall Street Journal* slipping from his hands. But I gather my nerve, for I'm usually not shy around this grandpa, with his funny, crinkly face, his silly humor, his normal English.

"Grandpa," I say, tugging at his suit jacket. When his eyes open, I tell him about Confucius.

I thought he would laugh. But he doesn't. He stands up, his face angry. He turns his back and walks out of the room. At once I know my mistake has been huge, and I feel pain behind my eyes.

My Sailor
1948

As I rake leaves in the backyard, the wind whips up mini tornadoes around me, and a dream from the night comes. I'm lost for a moment, stunned even. I drop my rake and slip back on a mound of leaves.

I'm in a phone booth with a sailor who's returned from the War. We're in love and whisper words about missing each other and loving forever. The sailor puts his muscley arms around my waist—that of the grown-up woman I've become. He touches my back, bare in my sundress, and I feel the scratch of his wool sailor suit. His fingers comb through my silky, pageboy hairdo. The phone booth is tight, but my sailor bends me backward and kisses me just as the sailor kisses the nurse in the famous end-of-the-war Times Square photo. I rub myself against him and feel my body parts heat up. I'm lost, dizzy, and gone. My face blends into his, my lips into his. This kiss from my sailor is deep, lustful. It's a kiss I've seen in the movies. Only this time I'm the woman, aroused, feeling it, loving it.

The cold wind snaps at my face, yet my cheeks flush hot and my ears tingle. I'm mystified, sharply aware that this dream is an impossibility. How could I experience a grown woman's sexuality—even in a dream—when I'm just a little kid?

I shake my head, pick up my rake, and scratch at the leaves. I will never tell anyone about the dream, not even Janice. I don't have the words. Yet I hold the dream close as a magical, spooky secret.

MY FISHNET TOP
1959

When I stroll down our backyard, there's a feeling of getting familiar again—trying to relax into the yard as I've done so many times before, loving the space, its lush green-ness reaching way back toward the pool, unused now, hidden behind bushes and a chain link fence. I'm home from college on spring vacation.

I don't carry anything with me, which is unusual, no book as an (unconscious) shield, no papers to write, no exams to study for. It's just me and the somewhat see-through, tan, fishnet top I'm wearing. I'm self-conscious about this new gift from a friend, and I'm not sure if it's stylish or ugly, or even OK to wear, since it's so loosely woven that you can see the outline of my bra. Yet I wear it.

Way down the slope, beneath the tallest oak, I lie flat on my back in the grass and fling my arms to my sides. Breathing deeply, I look up at the green and feel the sun flashing specks of warmth on my face. As I close my eyes, the blackbirds make their racket. Or are they crows?

Suddenly, my father is there, standing over me. I sense his presence and open my eyes. It's not unusual that he would walk down the backyard, checking the trees for bugs, for dying limbs, hanging branches, and the pool fence for break-ins. But it's unusual that he would startle me so, standing over me, so close. "Oh," I say. "It's you."

"So, it feels good to be home?" he asks. His glasses glint in the sun, and I can't see his eyes.

I sit up and then quickly pull myself to my feet.

"That's some top you're wearing." He shifts from one foot to the other.

"Yeah, I know. Someone gave it to me. I don't think I like it too much," I say.

His gaze is fixed on my breasts, fixated on my breasts. He doesn't turn his eyes away. Perhaps he says something else. Or maybe not. All I know is that he should have turned his eyes away by now. Should have. I cross my arms over my breasts. "I'd better go study," I say, turning toward the house.

"That's some top," he says again, louder, his tone lewd, as if he's suddenly slid out of his father persona into that of a creepy stranger, awkwardly picking up a honky-tonk woman in a bar, practicing his come-on. My face flushes. There's tightness in my throat, fear.

I rush up to the house.

This didn't just happen. This couldn't have happened.

He stays back, and from inside, I see him walk more around the yard, picking up stray rocks, fallen branches. I don't know what. The meticulous man. The careful man. Making sure nothing bad happens in the backyard.

SHOCK
1962

I drag the blue chaise into the still-hot, late-afternoon sun, closer to the house and spread my things around me in the grass—my tanning lotion, sun glasses, *Beginning Chinese* book, yellow pad, pens, cigarettes, matches, ashtray, and glass of iced coffee. I settle on the chaise, light up a Pall Mall, and open my textbook, exhaling a stream of smoke over the bold ink strokes. I must learn for tomorrow's quiz at Yale, my chosen summer distraction between college and graduate school.

How odd these characters! How difficult to learn!

I will not think about Margo upstairs.

With the pad on my knees, my pen poised, I slip into my study mind. The air around me softens into a protective cloud. My jaw relaxes.

I practice the pictograph for "roof" and the various elements I can write underneath it to form different meanings. I scratch the "roof" on my pad, then beneath it, the symbol for "woman," forming the character for "peace." An old-fashioned idea, I guess, the little woman under the roof, and all is well. It's easy to remember, but my roof is too wavy, my woman's elbows too sharp.

I will not think about Margo upstairs, her stringy, unwashed hair, the purple darkness around her frantic eyes, wandering my bedroom, asking again and again where her hairbrush has gone.

The symbol for "pig" is frilly and fancy, more like a skinny bird in a fright wig. When I sketch this "pig" under the "roof," the character means "family" or "home"—a sign of prosperity, says our instructor, Mr. Chin—a pig to sell in town, or ham to eat right at your table. A lucky family, indeed. Just like us, I think, in our big stone house, eating pork chops for dinner while Margo was falling apart in Boston, her mind exploded. I practice this character.

Now on to "tell." On the left, the symbol for "mouth" with dash-like words flowing out. On the right, an "ax." I don't get it. The power of words? Sharp like an ax?

Inside our stone house, words are hushed, rare. My parents don't discuss Margo's breakdown with me, or with anyone else that I can see. In 1962 it's not OK to have a crazy person in the family. The word "depression," though, slips out of their mouths and fills the rooms with gray, thick fear. And I know enough. Margo sent to Yale/New Haven mental hospital, then taken out by my psychiatrist father, brought home, and given shock treatments at his office by another doctor. Some afternoons, like today, I take her for shock and then bring her home to stay with me in my bedroom, upstairs.

I will not think about it.

I practice some Chinese sounds, but they connect to nothing. *Jia*, I say, *Xie, Xin, Chi.* I point to the characters and speak, point and speak, point and speak. My eyes close and my head falls back on the chaise, cheeks raised to the sun. I drift…

A car door slams. My father is home. I sit up, grab my pen, scratch anything on my pad. He strides onto the lawn near me, looks up at the roof, squinting in the sunlight at the loose drainpipe, a potential hazard.

"How's Margo doing?" he asks, scanning the roof.

"OK, I guess. She's up in my room." I hope these will be our only words. And they are. He goes up the stairs, in for his scotch and his nap before dinner.

My mother comes out while the roast cooks. She holds an iced tea and the *New York Times*. She's so thin. "Want anything from inside?" she asks. "More coffee? Cheese and crackers?"

"No, nothing," I say, scrunching into my study face, staring at my book.

She pulls a chair near mine, sits, and opens her paper.

"*Pa*," I say to myself. The sound for "fear." The "heart" symbol is on the left. On the right, the symbol for "white." Ah, the pale heart, the heart of white, the shocked heart, frightened into whiteness. I get this. I get this.

Allen Dickstein

I Could Not Speak

I WILL GET UP, I will get well, I will get over it, and I will get happy… eternally happy. This is what I want.

There is agony having an untold story inside me.

I wanted to speak, but I could not!

I wasn't taken by something. I wasn't flabbergasted. I wasn't surprised.

I could not speak. I could not express my feelings.

I want to be happy. I want to move forward! This is what I want.

An extremely adorable sweet and innocent three-year-old boy dressed in a sailor suit and leaning against the stark, cold brick of the two-story house.

It was an ominous house, metaphorically filled with frightening, sad remembrances of things past, holding on to me, not letting me go. Not letting me move from the dark, scary bleakness of the wall holding me emotionally steadfast.

The sweet sailor-suited little boy felt unloved, unwanted, intensely trapped by the sadness he felt as if truly cemented and attached to the cold, bleak brick wall.

He was an emotional prisoner, apprehensive about what would come next.

Could he move away from the emotional brick wall that held his mind and soul?

He knew he had a plethora of untold stories about his life, his young innocent life that caused him to experience so much sadness and pain at an early age when most young children were running around chasing butterflies.

He wanted desperately to speak, to shed the shackles that held his emotional body tightly to the cold, bleak brick wall.

His arms were raised above his head involuntarily attached to the brick wall, but this was only symbolic.

Yes, he was three years old and did not have the emotional fortitude to free himself from the wall, trapped, terrified, abandoned by all who knew him and those he thought loved him and those he wanted to love him.

He could emotionally move away from the wall and to be free, but he felt helpless and hopeless as if he existed in a world of nothingness.

How could this beautiful sailor-suited angel be free, be happy? Could he rid himself of this untold story?

Would he survive? Would his emotions allow him to be free and speak from his heart?

He knew he would get well! He knew life would take him away from the wall, far from the wall. Yes, he would have pain and sadness, but he knew he would be free from his painful past.

This little boy would one day find the emotional fortitude to get over it all, to feel alive, to be eternally happy, and to thrive. He would speak!

L'CHAIM

The clanging, charging cacophony of rolling tanks is seared into my brain. I am in emotional torment and hell. I want to retreat deep inside my soul and block out this doom and damnation.

I hear the sound of stomping feet hitting the pavement and now I see line after line of murderous marching machines hell bent on exacting fear and exulting in their victory.

They are triumphant throughout Eastern and Western Europe... big cities and towns and small villages.

No, I won't hail these venomous vultures. No, I won't bow before these brutal barbarians. No, I will not alter my way of life no matter what they forbid.

I am Jewish!

I must find a way to survive. Do I hide, do I run? How do I protect my family, my loved ones? Will I survive...will they survive? How will I not perish? How will I not suffer?

My tears belong to the dead and departed who so violently and valiantly fought for the city and country I love.

My heart is broken, my soul is terrified, but my spirit will not leave me without hope and I will not be cast into despair.

I want my enemy to be gone. I want to find ways to defeat them and push them into the sea and never again behold them.

I want to live! I want to grow old in peace. I want to watch my children grow and their children grow.

I will no longer shed tears for those brave souls who have perished fighting this manifold, murderous evil. They have no heart and no soul, and they care not for humanity.

I am Jewish!

I have lost contact with relatives. Fear and death have over taken me and control my mind.

Have they been murdered…have they been tortured…have they been annihilated? Have they been buried in the loneliness of nothingness?

How will I ever know where they are and if they are among the living?

I fear they are gone, never to be seen…victims of this hoard of evil who will stop at nothing to conquer and kill and wipe out an entire race, an entire religion, an entire people.

Deep in my heart I must believe that this evil will perish and I and my loved ones will survive.

I must believe they will live and continue new generations, new loves, new joys.

I will always look for them…

To Live…to Life!

My Love Lost

I was dying from a broken heart…this is what I came to understand about love lost. This extremely painful feeling affected my heart, my soul, my mind, and my body. Sometimes I wish we had never met. I wish we had not attended the same health club and had not seen each other or noticed each other...but we did.

I knew he loved me but could not really love me because he did not love himself. He did not have any positive feelings about himself except that he was very handsome and everyone looked at him and everyone wanted him. But he loved me as I loved him.

It was the raging 1980s...the AIDS epidemic! We had broken up, came back together, and broken up.

It was the month of January in 1985 when I saw him on the New York subway. I looked away because seeing his face increased my agony and mental anguish and I could not deal with this. He walked over to me and quietly said, "I have AIDS." I burst into tears not caring who saw me.

I said, "We must be together." He wanted that too. We knew how much we had always loved each other and that we never wanted to be apart. This is the love we shared and the bond that would bring us together.

The first time we saw each other after meeting on the subway, we sat at opposite ends of the sofa in his apartment not daring to move closer. But slowly we did and our hearts poured out torrents of tears and feelings. We remained together what seemed like eternity.

When he got worse, he sold his apartment and moved in with me. While this was agony, it was also joy in spite of what we both endured. I took care of him night and day and even learned to cook Macrobiotic food, which many believed would cure this horrendous disease.

People said to me, "How can you care about him...how can you be so loving and giving?" My response was simple...love is love and that's it, no matter how much emotional pain I feel. I know it's real! He knows his love for me is real!

As the next two years progressed, he became worse. One day in the AIDS unit of the hospital, he asked me what I felt about his dying. I did not know how I managed to be strong and as calm as possible. I told him that in spite of our highs and lows, he made it possible for me to know what it was like to be in love and that it was OK for him to let go and not to suffer any longer. He was happy and said that he hoped, in time, that I would meet someone else and again find love.

Two weeks later he died in my arms.

I knew I had to go forward…I knew it would not be emotionally healthy for me to build a shrine to him…I knew in time that I would meet someone else and fall in love…this I did. I made him happy.

My love lost was my love found.

TRAPPED

I was trapped and could not get out. I screamed, I cried, I began to suffocate.

Help me someone, help me. But no one came.

I can't breathe. I'm going to die alone, completely trapped and powerless.

It was brutally hot…ninety-five degrees.

I shook. I grabbed at my clothes. I began pulling off my shirt thinking it would help me breathe. I had no means of communication…no cell phone, no nothing.

The walls closed in and my level of fear was unbearable. I could not stop hyperventilating. I could not stop having a panic attack.

Suddenly, miraculously, my fear and panic turned to rage, utter complete rage. I began screaming every four-letter word possible. I became verbally violent and wanted to smash everything around me… of course there was nothing around me.

Why was I alone? Why could no one be with me to comfort me, to quiet me? I so desperately needed assurance and reassurance.

Then without warning, my world began to move and the space surrounding me seemed to be speeding upward.

I urgently grabbed at anything, hoping desperately to protect myself from collapsing, falling, hitting my head, my neck, my entire being.

I had no idea this simple movement would cause chaotic terror.

As Oscar Wilde so eloquently said, "everything is dangerous my dear fellow"…my dear Allen.

Suddenly everything stopped, a door opened, and out I jumped without a moment's hesitation.

Yes, I survived and my life would be worth living.

I was safe but I know more danger will be thrust upon me…today, tomorrow, next week…who knows when.

The elevator did not claim me!

Isaac Dimitrovsky

A series of memories of my father, some
of which have a supernatural
flavor disturbing to a rationalist like myself:

Heh-ahvar ayin;	The past is gone;
Heh-ahtid adayin;	The future has not yet come;
Heh-hoveh keheref ayin;	The present–blink and it's done;
Im kehn, deh-ahgah meenayin?	So, where is worry from?
Ibn Ezra	

MY FATHER, HAIM ZALMAN DIMITROVSKY, was a formidable Talmudic scholar. He had an amazing mind—its greatest strengths were memory, pattern recognition, and the ability to maintain focus on a project for long days and years. One of his major works was the reconstruction of a lost edition of the Talmud that had been printed in Spain before the expulsion of the Jews in 1492. He put it together from fragments of pages found among discards and recycled book bindings scattered around the world. Another work that took up much of his life and was still occupying him when he died was an authoritative collection of the responsa (written rulings/opinions in response to questions) of a thirteenth-century Jewish sage known as the Rashba (abbreviation of Rabbi Shlomo ben Aderet), who wrote thousands of responsa to questions from far-flung Jewish communities across Europe and Asia Minor.

Below are some personal memories of my father, spanning about fifty years.

When I was a small child I had a bad dream one night. My father appeared in the dream and said, "Go away, bad dream!" And the bad dream spread its wings and flew away.

In 1986, the Mets went to the World Series. I was a pretty intense Mets fan, and I was really nervous before game six of the series, because they were down three games to two and facing elimination if they lost. My father saw how nervous I was, and he took me aside and told me, "Don't worry, they're going to win—and it will be a miracle." For the skeptical, I should add that this is the only time I can remember my father making a sports prediction. The next day, the Mets won game six in the most improbable comeback in World Series history, after trailing by two runs with two outs, two strikes on the batter, and nobody on in the bottom of the ninth. It was almost an anticlimax when they won the series the next day.

When I was going to college I would often stay late at the Hebrew University campus in Jerusalem and then walk home in the wee hours. Once he asked me if I wasn't afraid of encountering *sheydim* (Yiddish/ Hebrew for demons or spirits). It seemed to me that he was at least a little serious about the question.

He consumed large amounts of sugar—he drank instant coffee all day and would put what seemed like eight or ten teaspoons of sugar in each cup. I remember once he gave me some fatherly advice about how lots of sugar helped you think. He also recommended burned foods for improving memory. He didn't seem to suffer any health consequences from the sugar—he never became diabetic or even gained much weight. I hope I inherited those genes, because I did get the sweet tooth.

He had a quality of extreme focus that I've seen in other people who are very good at something. It reminded me of the episode in *A Study in Scarlet* when Dr. Watson was incredulous to find out that Sherlock Holmes didn't know the earth went around the sun:

"But the Solar System!" I protested.
"What the deuce is it to me?" he interrupted impatiently. "You say that we go round the sun. If we went round the moon it would not make a pennyworth of difference to me or to my work."

My father wasn't that extreme—he did have some interest in politics, sports, and so on, but he had a considerable amount of that focus. I remember once we went to a Charles Schwab branch and talked to a nice young broker for an hour or so. Then when the broker left the room for a minute, my father turned and whispered to me, "Is that Mr. Schwab?" Another time, my mother and he were trying to learn how to use a computer. So they had someone from the computer store come by to give them a lesson. He taught them for a couple of hours, and my mother was finding it hard to follow, but she saw that my father, who had an impressively scholarly manner, kept nodding gravely like a chess master seeing a difficult combination—so she figured he had it covered. Then after the guy left she asked my father if he'd understood all that, and he replied, "Kin ein vort nicht" (Yiddish for "Not a single word").

Sometimes people would come to ask my father for an opinion on some point of Jewish law as it applied to their lives. As far as I heard, he always tried to find the most lenient possible interpretation of the law—the one that the person asking could fulfill with the least trouble.

An hour or two before he died, my father called me from the hospital. We talked for a little while. He told me that he hoped I could accomplish everything that I wanted to and that they loved me very much.

A few months after he died, I had a dream where I was walking with my father. We came to a street crossing and I turned to him and started crying. He asked me why I was crying, and I told him, "Because you're gone, and this is the only way I can talk to you now." He looked at me and said, "You know—when you cry, I can hear you."

HAIKU EDITORIALS ABOUT DONALD TRUMP

Around the beginning of 2016, for reasons uncertain, I felt compelled to start writing haiku that summarized the daily editorials in the New York Times *and* Wall Street Journal. *It was unexpectedly challenging to cut through the convoluted thickets of verbiage that often form on those pages and extract the main thought from each editorial. Below is a sample of some historical interest—I wrote these haiku as Donald Trump's presidential run started to roll. Despite being far apart politically, both the* New York Times *and* Wall Street Journal *demonstrated a hearty contempt for Trump, for different reasons. Reading through these, one can feel in quick succession the emotions that must have passed through those boardrooms: denial and contemptuous dismissal, slowly dawning realization, bargaining, and, finally, stunned disbelief.*

NYT, 12/31/2015: **The More We Poll, the Less We Know**
　　Trump brags about polls
　　early, unreliable.
　　Don't fret until March.

WSJ, 1/28/2016: **The Leap of Trump**
　　His voters want hope
　　but they should reconsider.
　　Trump is a black swan.

WSJ, 1/30/2016: **The Sanders-Trump Fuel**
　　What's behind their rise?
　　A decade of subpar growth
　　caused by Obama.

WSJ, 2/16/2016: **Donald Trump's MoveOn.org Moment**
　　He repeated that
　　crackpot left-wing theory:
　　Bush lied on Iraq.

NYT, 2/18/2016: **South Carolina's Legacy, Exploited by Trump**
　　Racism still endures.
　　Many Trump fans wish the South
　　won the Civil War.

NYT, 2/18/2016: **Pope Francis at the Border**
brings hope and solace
as GOP brings fear and
Trump, deep ignorance.

WSJ, 2/22/2016: **America's Moment of Trump**
Trump's winning—will we
jump off that cliff? There's still time.
Switch to Rubio.

NYT, 2/28/2016: **Donald Trump and Chris Christie Start a Bully Bromance**
sweaty Trump embrace
medley of playground insults
make him Transport Sec.?

NYT, 3/2/2016: **The Party of Trump, and the Path Forward for Democrats**
GOP's reeling
stuck with bombastic liar.
Clinton pulls ahead.

NYT, 3/3/2016: **Donald Trump and Reconstruction-Era Politics**
Trump flirts with the Klan
and with other extremists
profits from race hate.

WSJ, 3/3/2016: **Trump's Pottery Barn GOP**
He's been winning by
fracturing the GOP
can still be denied.

NYT, 3/4/2016: **Mitt Romney Aims at Donald Trump, Hits G.O.P.**
Rambling indictment
blasts Trump for things GOP
has long been doing

WSJ, 3/7/2016: **The GOP Race Isn't Over**
Forrest Trump's support
erodes as he's vetted—will
we buy those chocolates?

NYT, 3/9/2016: **Trying to Read Donald Trump, in Translation**
Trump alarms Europe.
They have had some bad times with
right-wing populists.

WSJ, 3/10/2016: **Hillary's Michigan Droop**
Dems shouldn't Trump-gloat.
Voters dislike Clinton too,
almost as badly.

WSJ, 3/12/2016: **The Donald and The Barack**
Obama led to
Trump, through nasty tactics, and
slow-growth policies.

NYT, 3/15/2016: **The Trump Campaign Gives License to Violence**
This year's George Wallace
vile Presidential campaign
stirs up viciousness.

WSJ, 3/16/2016: **Kasich into the Breach**
  Rubio goes down.
  It's Kasich's turn to fight Trump
  to the convention!

WSJ, 3/17/2016: **Trump's Unification Tour**
  pulls out of debate and
  threatens convention riots.
  A brain trust of one.

Judith Elaine Halek

LOST AND FOUND

I wander at five
Skipping down an unknown path
Smells of lilac call.

Mindless walking far
Lost in the greens and the sounds.
Small hands on huge pines.

Darkness begets light.
Awareness turns into fear.
Where am I going?

Search parties come out.
Name echoes throughout the woods,
Falling on deaf ears.

I roam further.
Playful bright lights bob midair
Like magical friends.

Howling pierces cut.
My flesh spikes goose flesh tenfold.
Will I live or die?

My tummy turns up.
My head spins out of control.
Further, further gone.

The tears know to come.
My body shakes and quakes now.
Anticipation.

Blinding lights appear
Through the dark, dense forest green
Ringing out loud cries.

"Judy, Judy, girl,"
Judy, Judy where are you?"
Short chubby legs run

Toward a welcome.
Warm embrace, kisses, and hugs
Melt all fears and pain.

Away dark dungeon
Away scary sounds and smells
Into sweet safety.

More tears and warm milk
Clean clothes, hamburgers, and fries
The lost girl is found.

Panic is now gone.
From family and good friends
Relief resonates.

All slumber deeply,
With unified family
Back home, safe and sound.

Fate in Its Finest Moments

Frantic, sweaty and late for a significant job interview, Howard blundered uptown toward 143rd Street and Broadway. "Where am I? Did I get off too soon? Was the appointment at 159th Street, not 143rd Street?" His mind scrambled as he looked at the unreadable directions scribbled on the crumpled, sweaty piece of paper in his clenched palm. If he's going to make the interview on time, he had to hurry.

In a haze, trying to get his bearings, he swiftly turned his head right, left, uptown, then downtown. The quick movements pulled

Howard off his center, and he stumbled slightly and slipped off the curb into the street, barely missing an oncoming honking cab, as the driver screeched and swerved off to the left. Like a panther sensing danger, his agile body angled out of the way, and he fell onto the sidewalk, slamming the right side of his body against a hard traffic-light fixture.

His best interview suit was soiled and his right pant leg was torn by the fall. Pain seared through his right leg. Covering the brightness of the sun with his left hand over his brow, Howard peered through squinted eyes and saw a few people running to his aide. A gentleman, around his age, in a suit, trench coat, and hat got to him first. Howard looked at him with wide, bulging eyes wondering where the hell he is.

The young man sensed, Howard's disorientation, with light humor laughingly blurted out, "Hey Buddy, do you want to get to the other side of the earth? Do you want to go to California? Come on, let me help you up."

"Isn't this New York?" Howard screamed back. "The other side of the earth is not California. What are you trying to do you maniac, mess with my head you idiot?" Flustered and bewildered Howard starts swinging at the outsider trying to assist him.

In an outbreak of confusion, two strangers find themselves engaged in a palm-slapping tango. The scene of two gentlemen in suits, hats, and trench coats battling it out on the streets of the New York City's cement jungle looked absurd to the few bystanders. To amplify the commotion, the sounds of the subway cars clanged by with a deafening screech of metal on metal.

"Hey, hey, hey, relax buddy. I'm trying to help you out," the Good Samaritan screamed.

"Oh yeah? Well I don't need your kind of help," Howard battled back continuing to punch the air.

A flurry of limbs and fabric continue. It became quickly evident to the onlookers and the men that neither of them would fair well in a boxing match. In the midst of their amateur tussle, even their hats continued to stay engaged on their heads. Howard continued to flail after the man who was trying to extricate himself from the scene, wondering if this crazy adult is going to harm him. At one point, Howard regained a bit of semblance and backed off. Out of nowhere, initiated from the depths of his being, Howard spontaneously began to laugh and laugh.

The Good Samaritan stepped back and, for a moment, watched Howard wondering what he was going to do next. Caught up in the absurdity of the situation, he began to laugh. Both men dropped to their knees onto the hard concrete, holding their bellies, laughing in tandem at the ridiculousness of the scene.

Howard never made it to the interview that day, but something more significant occurred. He began a friendship that would last the next forty years.

In Memory of Walter

Walter was diagnosed before me. Yet, his immune system had been more compromised than mine. Years earlier he'd experienced autoimmune challenges and went through a period of touch and go with his health. He made it through to the other side, but later, when the new diagnosis appeared, his reserves had become exhausted.

Most people would like to be remembered after they transition out of their body, and Walter was someone you'd never forget.

It's been months since his passing, and many of us feel him sitting on the stoop in front of the building with his morning Joe. He had the kind of face that welcomed friend and foe. Always observing, he would acknowledge you with a nod, smile, or a humorous comment. Walter held himself with confidence and pride whether he dressed casually or dressed to the nines. And though there were days he appeared spent from the daily radiation treatments, I would see him leaning against the outside of our building, bathed in sunlight, like a cat curled up in it's favorite spot, his head tilted back, eyes closed, and a smile across his mouth.

My visits to Walter were a convenient two flights below. During his last months, I was recovering from the effects of my chemo treatments and surgeries and I would visit him in his apartment. We serenaded each other with our outrageous medical yarns, all the while busting a gut when comparing who looked better bald.

As I sat perched at the end of his bed, rubbing and kneading his feet with a lavender-laced foot crème, I watched him become lost in the ecstasy of relief from sore, stiff muscles, tendons, and ligaments. He'd close his eyes and smile with periodic moans of dreamy delight, inferring "never stop." During these quiet moments with intermittent long, low sounds, I remember envying Walter. His time on earth was waning and I knew mine was not. The collapse of my careers and uncertainty of my future spun me into a tale of terror, making me desire the definitiveness of Walter's demise.

My logical brain screamed inside, "How can you feel jealous of someone dying and guilty of not wanting to live?" These concepts would continue to haunt me for many months. While everyone around me commented on how "wonderful" I looked and said, "isn't it great you are cancer-free," all I wanted to do was curl up in a hole and die. The truth was, whoever I was before the diagnosis was gone and now the emergence of what and who was next was paralyzing.

Walter would sometimes speak of what he would do when he got himself strong enough to get out of bed. I would wonder what it would be like to be out of body and on the other side of this time, space, and reality. We were living in our delusions.

The day Walter died, I was sitting in a local Starbucks reading and writing. One of the tenants in our small Upper Westside building came up to me and asked if I knew Walter had passed early that morning. I hadn't. I thanked him for letting me know and left the coffee shop to go back and sit in Walter's apartment. As I drifted down Broadway, two blocks to our apartment building, a pang of nostalgia swelled from the depth of my belly as I recalled our last encounter.

There were so many people going in and out taking care of Walter, and his apartment door was unlocked all hours of the day and night. Today was no different. Even though his body had been removed, the door remained unlatched.

I slipped into the vacant space and immediately felt the fullness of his presence. I could smell his scent, feel his energy, and recognize his notorious smile while gazing at the portrait of his father on the bedroom wall. His father had turned ninety, five months prior to Walter's death. Fortunately, Walter was able to travel the hundred miles to surprise his father for his birthday celebration. At Walter's memorial, I approached his father and graciously introduced myself. I looked into his moist, swollen, bloodshot eyes and gently shook his large, thick, strong hand.

"You raised a fine man. He was loved by many," was all I managed to blurt out.

He smiled weakly, thanked me softly. and with cane in hand continued down the aisle to his designated seat, surrounded by an entourage of protective, tearful family. I could not stop thinking how many times I'd heard the phrase, "A parent should never have to bury their child."

Back in Walter's bedroom, I became Alice In Wonderland walking through the looking glass, captivated by the two o'clock shadowy light seeping through the half-closed gray sheers, orchestrating a surreal, magical moment. Everything seemed illuminated with a silvery hue. The beams of golden sunlight filtered through the faded curtains and captured billions of speckled stardust, making the room come alive with movement.

As I drank in this suspended time and space, I came to understand what it means to be living alone and dying alone. It was palpable and registered with a heavy, empty pressure in the center of my chest. I took a deep breath out and remembered that I was alive and alone, yet alive. Right now this was about Walter and giving him due respect.

I sat in the chair I always sat in, across from him on the bed. I slipped off my shoes and tucked my toes between the ancient mattress and box spring. I then proceeded to write my final good-bye. As I wrote, I heard sounds of dishes shuffling in the kitchen. A sign from Walter, the consummate chef, he was in the apartment. It made me smile.

I guess we're really never alone.

To My Beloved Walter

Walter was a man who embraced life richly.
He loved fully and lived freely.
He had a razor-sharp mind, even weeks before his passing.
He resided at the "end of the hall" on the 4th floor at 309,
Yet, his presence was felt throughout the building.
When passing Walter in the building,
On the elevator, or in the street,
There was always a welcoming look, touch, hug, or smile.
He extended his heart out to many
Because he cared for so many.
When something was said or done that elicited a spark,
His eyes would widen like saucers and
A tiny curl formed at the ends of his lips sug-
gesting the beginnings of a smile.
It was a contagious instant as everyone around him
Followed suit, with laughter as the end result.
Walter was a man who believed in
And honored God through his unique
And expressive ways.
Even though his body is gone,
The true essence of Walter resides
In the hearts of everyone he met.
What a gift you gave the world, Beloved Walter.
We love you, miss you, and know
Your memory lives on in the
Thousands of people you touched and
Made a "difference" in their lives,
By just "being," WALTER.

Diagnosis, Treatments, Post-Cancer

Inner self knows. I am dying. Wait long time. Go get tested. July 27, 2014. Ground zero news. Screamed over phone. Lymph nodes swollen. Round thirteen centimeters. Belly and pelvis. Kidneys are compromised. Vena cava crushed. Twenty-seven-year career. Gone to belly. No more service. No more babies. Time to stop.

Time for me. Time for truth. Time for emergency.

I live through. Six chemo treatments. Eight surgeries later. So much pain. Rite of passage. I am lost. I lose hair. I lose weight. I gain everything. New life lease. New pure potential. Moment to moment. There is light.

People fall away. More death around. I feel abandoned. I lose faith. I find faith. Community helps me. Caring Bridge Blog. Give Forward Campaign. Google Calendar helps. Cancer Care resourceful. Gilda's Clubhouse rocks. Enjoy humorous YouTube. Flowers are sent. Gifts are received. Emails are abundant. Phone calls appreciated. Bone broth cherished.

I need aloneness. Difficult for visitors. Difficult for me. I organize paperwork. I organize appointments. I organize money. Multitude of thanks. Twenty-nine, three-ring binders. I am exhausted.

Dolly sends cards. Sister Mary visits. Deb attends chemo. Susan cooks Sundays. Laura writes notes. Teri supports shots. Ken shoots photos. Myla documents henna. I am blessed.

Writing is manna. Emily's class lifesaving. Writing becomes medicine. Writing allows healing. Belly releases book. Book reveals voice. The Write Treatment.

Caterpillar to butterfly. Birth Maven completes. Cancer Thriver begins.

No hair before. Now have hair. Blonde hair before. Charcoal-gray now. Standing alone naked. Sharing deepest truths. I breathe deep. Hundred times daily. I am alive.

Lessons I learn: Ask for help. Receive that help. Allow my vulnerability. Heal with family. Heal with friends. Heal with self. Learn to love. Learn to be. Stay in the moment. Let go past. Release all attachments. One foot forward. Find the trust.

Allow the change. Express my fear. Keep tears flowing. Pray every day. Thanks and gratitude. Listen to body. Remember, I AM. Belly laughs help. Therapy can help. Find my THRIVE.

Not finished yet. What will come? Who can say. Only time will. Somehow reinventing myself. Reconnect with God. Create new dialogue. Scared like hell.

Sixty years old. November 8th birthday. Butterfly Exhibition experience. Marks regenerative Scorpio. I am newness. Out of chrysalis. Forming new self. Dinner with friends. Toasts all around.

Here I go! One—two—three. I am free. Finding my passion. Giving of service. Loving what is. Letting Divine lead.

Jacqueline Johnson

DAY OF DIAGNOSIS: JUNE 23, 2010

TIME BEFORE THE APPOINTMENT:
IT WAS WEDNESDAY, JUNE 23, 2010. As the sun rose over Decatur, Georgia, I awakened to the sound of birds singing and the sweet fragrance of the magnolia trees just outside my window drifted into the room. Elsewhere in the northern most part of the country, the news reported severe weather events of winds, flooding, and funnel clouds.

I began my day with my usual daily routines amidst a mix of unacknowledged emotions. A part of my morning activity was Bible reading, meditation, and prayer. This morning's daily reading from my devotional was titled, "Brier and Buttercups", the accompanying scripture was Acts 14:1-22. It spoke of miracles and the faith to be healed. How ironic and comforting this meditation and prayer time was for me.

This day was to be filled with events for me; it was the day I determined to get the results of my biopsy. Immediately after the biopsy, I had scheduled vacation days. I had informed Dr. Candor my plans and that I would not be able to receive any direct calls during my time away. It was purely coincidental. Three phone messages were left by Dr. B. Candor on my voice mail that my biopsy results were in with instructions to call her office and schedule an appointment. I had made numerous phone calls to schedule an appointment in response to the urgency in her southern drawl. I was feeling very anxious and frustrated as each attempt failed. I decided I would walk in and state that I was there at Dr. Candor's request. On the voice message, she told me to tell the receptionist I was to be worked in; somehow they didn't get the memo and would not give me an appointment immediately. I was anxious to get my results. I felt helpless not hopeless.

TRAVEL TO THE OFFICE:
I went on to work in the morning and planned to go to Dr. Candor's office at lunch time since it was five minutes walking distance from my office. That did not give me much time to think or feel about what to expect from the biopsy report. I was feeling angry and uncertain about this doctor and how she ran her practice. There seemed to be a lack of communication between her and her staff.

ARRIVAL AT THE OFFICE AND THE ROOM AT THE OFFICE:
I arrived at doctor's office and informed the receptionist I was there to see Dr. Candor at her request and asked her to announce my arrival. After hanging up the phone, the receptionist said, "Dr. Candor said you can come in." As I walked toward Dr. Candor's office, I recalled the events of my first visit for the biopsy. Dr. Candor's attitude was distant and uncaring. We sat in her darkened office. A sole desk lamp penetrated the darkness. I felt as if I was being interrogated by a law-enforcement agent firing questions at me and not allowing time for proper answers. To add to the tension, she spoke in a very thick and distinctive southern drawl, as an African American woman; it was daunting. The intense pain of the biopsy and her very discouraging words in the midst of her performing the biopsy all came flooding back to my memory. I felt ignorant as I couldn't answer the questions and traumatized by the way the biopsy was performed in a cold, dark-ened examination room. The room somehow reflected the personality of this doctor. Dr. Candor and a nursing assistant were standing out-side her office waiting for me. She had a folder in her arms, and with a pleasant expression on her face, she gestured with her other hand to redirect me to another office. I followed her past the examining room where the biopsy had been done. The nursing assistant followed behind me. We walked into an office space nicely decorated and with a glass wall, allowing for the entrance of the warmth and brightness of the sun. As we entered the room, I wondered about the purpose of the nursing assistant's presence. I was not asked permission to have a stranger in the room, nor how I felt about having my personal and private health information heard by a stranger. The feeling of peace and calm in the room pervaded the atmosphere, and my thoughts of discomfort dissipated. This was the telling room, the room where I would hear words to live by or die by.

GETTING THE NEWS:
We were all seated. Dr. Candor behind the desk, the nursing assistant at her side, and I with my back to the warmth of the sun's rays. Dr. Candor opened the folder that contained the pathologist's report and read to me the following words, "There is a low grade endometrial adeno sarcoma, also known as uterine cancer." I listened as she said the words, thinking let it be an operable benign tumor; adeno sarcoma is not what I want to hear. I knew enough to know those words were dangerous. I felt disbelief and an uncertainty about what it all meant for my life. It was as if Dr. Candor had slapped my face, and it stung.

I was in a frozen time warp, in a wind funnel. In the distance I could hear Dr. Candor saying, "If she had to deliver any news, this was the best of the worst kind of news." She was going to refer me to a gynecology oncologist, and she suggested that a robotic surgery be performed to remove the tumor. The only problem was the surgeon she wanted to do the procedure had relocated to Florida, so she'd have to look for someone else. Restrictions after surgery included not driving for six weeks. She asked if I had support here, I answered, "No, my family is in New York." This answer to her question brought me back to the room. I said, "Dr. Candor, I am moving to New York where my support is. I appreciate everything you've done for me." I shook her hand and walked out of the office.

LEAVING THE OFFICE:
I felt I had regained some control over my life, although it seems I had lost control of my body to cancer. I summoned some courage, maybe it had to do with my time spent in meditation and prayer. I could think about a plan and strategy to get to New York as I walked home.

ARRIVAL AT HOME:

Once home, I called Kim, my counselor, and discussed the situation. By this time the storm of harsh reality arrived; my eyes flooded and the tears ran down my face like a broken dam. Emotions swept over me like a hurricane. I had managed to sit and calmly receive this life-changing news, keeping my emotions pent up. Kim was not available. Once I composed myself, I called my insurance company and asked for a female gynecology oncologist at Beth Israel Medical Center in New York. They gave me a name and a phone number. I called the number, Rene answered the phone, and I was able to arrange an appointment. This allowed me time to book a flight and tie up loose ends at work. I would need to take a leave of absence request from my job. The strength welled up from within as I prepared to call and tell my children. Kim suggested I tell them before I arrived in New York. She was right. I felt relieved, helpless not hopeless.

I have lived to tell this story. I realize the brevity of life, whether in good health or not so good health. I ask you the question, what in life is ever secure?

THE BOY IN THE STRIPED TEE SHIRT

One autumn day I was walking along the city streets with my camera in hand. There was no plan of photographing anything or anyone in particular. I noticed a young boy, maybe preadolescent, playing with some other boys about the same age. He had a face that transcended time, and he seemed to represent generations of young African American males.

I was suddenly aware of the variation of horizontal stripes on his shirt, which contrasted with the vertical iron bars on the fence he had posed himself against. Judging by the chain tightly wrapped around the gate entrance and locked shut with a padlock securely in place, the owner of the property obviously wanted the assurance of keeping trespassers out and safety within. There was something soft and innocent in his face.

Our eyes had met, and I approached him to ask if he would oblige me by posing for a picture. He agreed and maintained his pose. As I looked into the lens of the camera to shoot the picture, so much about history rang out, and yet I was intuitively aware of his story. As I studied his face, his eyes looking directly into the camera gave the impression that there was not an object between us. There was a reflection of wisdom and contentment exuding from them. The slight smile seemed to express humble self-confidence. The right hand posed over his head holding onto a cold metal fence post seemed to signify he had a grasp on his life. He was making a statement that he was in front of the bars, not behind them. There were no chains shackled around his hands and feet but around the gate. His wry smile said, "I am a conqueror."

Consequently, his pose reminded me of an action hero. I pictured this champion, who was reaching behind to pull forth an arrow from a quiver to be placed in a bow or for a shield slung low across his back. Whatever it was he was reaching for, he had the appearance of a warrior ready for anything, ready for the future. He had put the cold, unfeeling, and unrelenting oppressors behind him and was not at all intimidated by anyone or anything, and he allowed me to record it all through my steady lens.

Melody Johnson

LOTUS POSITION

The first time I tried,
My mother was already midway
Into her mantras,
The eye-burning incense floating
Its prayers to some heaven.

I wanted to be like Wanda Watkins,
Who could do the splits both ways,
Crotch flat on the gymnasium floor
Armless cartwheels, somersaults
Head of the cheerleading squad.

You have to learn to breathe.

My pretzel legs wished themselves into a treble clef,
Toes playing peek-a-boo,
Feet finding resting place on thighs.

I got it on my eighteenth try.
Nineteen if you don't count,
The time my legs fell asleep.
One hour. One hour. Morning. Night.
A mother's pride.
A daughter's perfect posture.

I could only wonder after that
How Wanda Watkins could be free
From these straight stretching mornings
Free from ankle bones on hardwood floor. Pain
Her savior never asked of her.

3131 LAKE BOONE TRAIL

If you ask me, Carolina sweat
Is the absolute sweetest the way it drips
From dark brows to salty eyelids,

Stings swirled with jasmine, mimosa,
Sticky spinsters swoon from scents of magnolia.

Any summer, any Carolina August
It's so still you can hear your neighbor's heart beating, especially just
before a hurricane—
And I promise: there will always be a hurricane.

No one moves that last week in summer.

No fool dare stand on the wrong side of a screened-in porch
But twirls, celebrating Moon, Stars fan themselves into fantasies:
Trickling, clear creeks over collarbones,
Pine forest blown breezes through dampened hair
With crawfish-catching, crocus-crushing—
Cool.

A Morning in Seoul

It was the bluest sky she'd ever seen on such a crisp autumn morning
where, already, the golden leaves on the large gingko tree were begin-
ning to quiver with life again, shaking like nervous children on their
first day of school. Sprouting from the mulch across the widowed
auntie's house were young hibiscus flowers, as if in daily ritual, rais-
ing their heads to the morning sun. Kyung-soon woke up and could
see her cloud-white breath as she exhaled near the cracked window
by her bed, hearing the sounds of village women gossiping over the
usual things. Yesterday, the chatter was about the summer trip they
had made to Busan and how they could afford to send only four of
the women from town to visit the coast and watch the seaweed divers
from the country's southernmost shore.

Some of the women were still angry that they were not chosen to go. "All my long life and I've never seen Busan and its deep blue water," complained the old grandmother, who walked with a reed to hold her brittle body up for many years now and would likely have made everyone wait endlessly for her three steps to catch up with their ten. Her skin as thin as rice paper showed mostly blue lines and shriveled sections that were just like crumpled paper meant to be thrown away. This morning's gossip was how, if Mr. Kim were still alive, he would not have doubled his market prices as his son, Bae-chuk, had done just two weeks after his father's death. "Five thousand won used to buy all the vegetables, rice, and fish to last me a whole week," exclaimed the widowed auntie. "Now, Bae-chuk is charging eight thousand won for the same because he knows the rich Americans will pay instead of buying that canned food at their commissary. For them, those prices are like small change, but how will we keep up with prices like that with no work available to us since they came back?"

All the aunties in the village offered their opinions to the widow's comments, the old short-haired auntie sternly reminding them as always: "First the Japanese, then the Chinese, and now, all these *leftover* Americans coming back and forth from Vietnam, like we are their private hotel! They plowed over our rice paddies and replaced them with their army buildings, tents, and now that airfield! That airfield's space was a village in itself years ago..." With all the babble and nods of agreements just after, it was hard for Kyung-soon to make out exactly what followed until the eldest auntie, Donut Mama-san, named so because her husband was the only donut vendor for many miles, raised her hand and spoke loudly above the others, her words as broad and noticeable as her too-large face that stood on such a slender frame of a body. Some children in the village called her "bighead" behind her back, but Kyung-soon was schooled by her mother to not insult or make fun of others' defects: "We simply walk farther to the Park family market so that Bae-chuk sees that we refuse to pay the higher prices he has set…and while the vegetables are not as fresh there, over a few days' time he will lower his prices again to honor his father's wishes." His father's wishes held sacred by the old village were simply to keep a friendly, loyal business as he had done for thirty-six years—after all, it was under the father's watchful eye, wasn't it, that the business became the most profitable one in the village, remember? Manage with a good heart to keep us returning. And to think, Bae-chuk breaking from the forty-nine days of proper mourning by reopening the shop to make money as soon as he can! His father could not possibly cross over the peaceful way into the new life with this greed of his son taking over. Donut Mama-san was well respected by the village women, and it was to her they turned for solving so many of their everyday problems: "My husband comes home every night with whiskey on his breath! He spends our last won buying his friends drinks at the tavern!" To this, Donut Mama-san responded with her usual solution for unruly husbands: "You need to keep a *cleaner* house and be a better wife. Never interrupt him when he speaks. This way your husband will want to come home to you and not stay out all hours of the night…"

Yes, every day it was the same chatter, to include the long-time problem and shame of the American soldiers sleeping overnight at the houses of some of the *business girls*, as they called themselves, but today was a special day Kyung-soon waited weeks for because her best friend, her *only* friend, Naida, would be going away to another village called America, and it was a place that was far, far away from what both girls' mothers described. Kyung-soon would go to Naida's house, where all the plentiful good food, sweet buns, and candy would be laid out on a table because of this special going away, along with toys and clothes that Naida would be unable to take with her. Naida's mother promised she would have better toys and clothes in America, and what's more, she would finally be able to go to school there.

A yellow-haired soldier, whose wife was waiting for him in America, chose Naida to become his 'doption daughter, and while many mothers would be so sad to give away their children, Kyung-soon thought it ridiculous for any mother to give her child away to a complete stranger. Naida's mother cried tears of joy when she knew that her daughter would no longer have to wander the streets begging from the local police officers or the soldiers in the camp. So far as Kyung-soon could figure out, 'doption daughters were not at all like real daughters but were loved and cared for just the same.

Because of this festive day, Kyung-soon could skip going to the soldiers' camp, waiting for the strange-looking men in green to pass out Chiclets or Hershey bars to stave her hunger for that particular day. Sometimes it was a coin or two they gave out instead, but Kyung-soon's mother scolded her many times for accepting anything more than food from these soldiers. When you disobey your mother's rules, so many loud words fill up the rest of the day telling you how you should be ashamed of yourself and what did your mother say so many times before? And especially do not accept money from the *business girls*, whom the mother described only as "bad women."

Her mother never understood that Kyung-soon enjoyed getting money the most, because this way, she could choose the food or candy *she* wanted instead of chewing Chiclets all day on an empty stomach. Occasionally, her mother would be able to bring home full meals in the early morning hours. Kyung-soon would make a game of holding the food on her tongue to savor the tastes of whatever beef, chicken, or dumplings were in the dish. Her favorite was salted mackerel mixed in the spicy, pungent cabbage stew.

This was the morning that Kyung-soon and Naida devoted to going to the playground, for the last time, near Naida's house. The girls would spin around on the rusty, squeaky merry-go-round and the sad, deflated balls all to themselves, just as most days, while the other children were in school. Let the grownups talk their endless talk. Argue more about Bae-chuk's market prices. The aunties will arrange all the spicy soups and pickled cabbage around their chatter, while she and Naida picked out which swings would swing them high enough to tickle their bellies to the loudest laughter on this decaying playground, where no other children came to play anymore, once they had built a better one in the schoolyard. The schoolchildren would look at them through the silver chain-linked fence that divided the playground from the main village street. As they walked in their blue uniforms and name tags with a funny writing on them, the boys and girls would glance and look quickly away from the two girls. And pretty little girls with their tight silky braids would walk singing a song about some rabbit and a child chasing it. *"San toki-toki-o…o derun ganun ya?"…Mr. Rabbit, where did you go?* Naida and Kyung-soon learned the whole song by hearing the younger schoolgirls singing it every day on the way to school.

Kyung-soon wondered if they looked so quickly away because the two girls themselves did not have proper uniforms to wear and the schoolchildren felt sorry for them or if the schoolchildren envied the fact that Kyung-soon and Naida could spend the day running and playing, tossing a ball, or making fortresses out of the tall bamboo reeds they were able to break off near the creek. Perhaps it was Naida's bright, green cat eyes. Naida's eyes reminded Kyung-soon of the no one's black cat that crept around the village nightly, getting fatter and fatter from the meals it made of everyone's garbage. Naida's eyes were as beautiful as that. And with her flow of brown hair, chestnut-colored like the beginning of each autumn harvest, Naida looked so incredibly different from Kyung-soon and the other girls in the village. Kyung-soon also saw these kind of eyes in the GI camp, where so many soldiers had eyes that were blue, green, and brown, faces speckled with red dots, and hair that was more yellow than the sun and more orange than the flame growing from the coals under the large basin her mother used to heat up their evening bath water.

Some soldiers had white or pink skin, some brown; either way Kyung-soon found it very hard to tell any of them apart. American soldiers were covered with too many colors that it confused Kyung-soon. Just like the business girls at night had confused her when they painted their eyelids and their lips a *naughty* red, as her mother would call it—just like the red lips of the women she and Naida had seen in an American magazine that Naida's mother snatched away before the girls had time to look at more pages.

For now, Kyung-soon's only worry was how to escape her chores and sneak out to spend the day with Naida. Kyung-soon's mother forbade her not to go to Naida's that day for fear the girl would learn more and more how to behave like an American girl. When mothers are squatting and busy washing vegetables in loud basins, they furrow their brows, thinking about so many important things, and then you can rush out of the house without them even knowing. Kyung-soon decided that as soon as she put on her day clothes, greeted her mother, and washed her face in the opposite basin of water near the wall on the porch being heated by the red-orange glow of the bundled twigs she gathered yesterday, she would simply walk beside her stone house and begin the short journey to Naida's home. Mothers could wash their vegetables all day long and even with children helping; they still squat for long hours cleaning more bean sprouts, more seaweed, more radishes, and whatever else was stacked up in the corner for that week's food. It seemed they always found yet another cabbage head or a mound of rice to wash, and Kyung-soon would not be missed.

Kyung-soon stood there silently and watched, as she had regularly done, watching her mother's hands plunging in and out of the cold ripples of water with a particular rhythm only the two were aware of—with the reflection of her mother's face in the brim of the silver basin, a reflection accented with short, accidental wisps of hair that fell forward, eventually framing her forehead. This was when her mother looked most beautiful, Kyung-soon thought, and *not* in the nighttime when she would paint all the many colors on her face, like the business girls her mother warned her about, and she changed her straight hair to curly. The neighboring auntie, whom all the children called "Emo" because she kept watch of many of the children in the area while their mothers were away, always stayed with the girl until the child fell asleep.

By morning, although her mother was so tired from her job, she still prepared the daily bone-marrow broth and rice for Kyung-soon to have ready when she woke up each morning. Her mother would then sleep much of the day away, telling the child which chores she had to do for which day. Sweep the part of the floor where the shoes are lined up. No, move the shoes away first. Wring out the rag, which always stayed afloat in clean water near the main door, and wipe the whole floor until there was no longer the color of dirt on the rag when finished. Change the water from dirty to clean again. Then the bed. There was then the parlor where there were the mud-caked, black combat boots of the soldiers, which should have been at the entrance of the main door. Her mother's friends would eventually explain to Kyung-soon about how Americans didn't know how to take off their shoes and were disrespectful of the floor space others ate and slept on. They did not know they were bringing the dirt of the cobblestone streets, the drool of dogs, and the spat-out chewing gum into such a clean place. Kyung-soon also made a little money helping out the washy-washy woman, as the American soldiers called her, but today she decided she would simply not show up to help deliver the laundry as she had done twice a week with her employer, who was miserly and paid her only three won for all the hard work she had done in one day. Small feet take much longer to travel, or didn't she know? Kyung-soon would always explain to washy-washy woman, as if it made any difference. The old woman began asking Kyung-soon to help her shortly after her daughter, who, for years, walked the camp by her mother's side taking in laundry, went away with one of those green soldiers. "Those dogs," she would often hear the laundress say, "they come and take everything away from us, even our daughters!" Washy-washy was among the group of women who gathered for the morning's gossip each day but her voice rarely stood out while Kyung-soon listened by her bed near the window. Washy-washy's face simply kept an angry look all the time, except when delivering the dry, folded clothes to the soldiers.

THE TOUR GUIDE

On the stifling hot bus we roll toward what looks like red heaven.
Or hell depending on how hydrated you were before boarding.
This sun can dry out a widow's grief.
The driver credits the Zuni tribe for the turquoise trinket he hands out.
Zuni tribe again for the brightly colored key ring given us
Texans in awe, not knowing what from what. (Just happens to be the state's colors the Zuni had in mind.)
So many stories, and we *want* to believe them, as humans *need* to believe.
Like the time I told my husband about the tribe of *Massa-chu*.
His "movie eyes" eager to know of their fall under the redcoats.
Their way of life taken. Their women, taken.

He needs to believe someone fought until the end,
Pressed on through musket fire, heads held high, our tribe of
Massa-chu
Back safe in Cambridge we play pretend for another eleven years,
His key ring and his rabbit's foot next to him in ICU.

MAZE

In the corners of my gaze I have four places
I ought to be at once:
In my auntie's prayers
My husband's embrace,
The infusion room, and Switzerland.

I stand in the middle, neutral,
Some soapbox in murky water,
Stepping stones too far apart to guide me.

I've just left my auntie's prayers
Feeling my way in the dark, arms stretched out,
Fingers fluttering for my husband's embrace.
My eyes strain and blink, strain, blink
In flashes of fluorescent blue on a radiologist's film.
Ears lean their way toward a lullaby of surgeon's voices,
Echoes of some party gone wrong the night before.
I twirl away from a loose embrace, stumbling
Into an infusion room.
Counting back from hundred, I feel the crisp Swiss cold at ninety-six.

THE PERIOD

Long before audiobooks, I would read my novels out loud
Into my cassette recorder
In the center of my Barbie mat,
Hoping one day to sell my tapes,
Five dollars per story.

I never got the whole book in,
Not even with side B.
Are you there, God? It's me, Margaret.
She grew up between the smell of new pages,
A time my parents wished I could stay small
In the center of my Barbie mat.
Danica called dibs when I got to the last page.

My mother was ashamed to talk of menses:
Had said *wait first until it comes.*
She would show me then.

Margaret and I learned the *Kotex* belt
Working the straps into the plastic clips.
We need protection.
Margaret was just a thought in some woman's head
A writer who allowed little girls to grow up.
My mother never talked about my menses.
Just saw the wads of napkins soaked with blood,
Hoped I was old enough to know when
I need protection.

WIGGLE ROOM

My hematoma
Pulses breathes waltzes with me
Even looks away

From husbands who curse
About the costs of living
And *now* this cancer?

Her gray eye tearing
Pus and fuss of memories
Told to remain shut!

A hole in my heart
That he did not cause this time,
This one will heal faster.

Cristina Liann

THE FAIR

"I JUST CAN'T BELIEVE IT! Were the judges blind?!" They barely gave a glance at Josie, but there they are, fawning over Tim's lamb. Well Josie was a lamb once too. She's just a little older and bigger'n Tim's. My daddy let me keep her and raise her just for this Fair.

Every day I got up early to feed and clean her. Josie even learned a few commands; that's how smart she is, but the judges didn't seem impressed when I showed that. I can't say anything 'cause it'll make the situation worse, but I'm not happy. What's so special about Tim's lamb anyway?! It just looks fluffier 'cause it's younger. Look at my Josie—she's so clean and smells so good today. I gave her a nice brushing and that made her just as pretty as that dumb ol' little lamb. "Dang! This pop just tastes flat now." Got no place to put it so I have to just stand an' hold it.

"Wait!" One of those judges just looked on over here. Aw…well, they moved away from Tim onto the girl next to him. She's got a fuzzy little lamb like Tim's, 'cept that it's got a ribbon around its neck, like that nursery rhyme. Now they're looking on over all of us. A couple of the judges come back. They give another look at Josie's hooves. I'm real glad I gave them a nice buff. Dang! I almost forget my manners when they speak to me, 'cause it's so close to the winning.

There they go. Now we've got to wait for their deciding. I see Daddy across the barn, but I don't want to look at him in the eye. Not until they do the announcing. A couple of the judges come over. Josie got a yellow ribbon! Third Place. "Dang!" I didn't get first, but neither did Tim. Tim only got fifth place—a pink ribbon. Some kid, older'n us got first. He's from over the next county.

I don't get awards too much. Now I can look at Daddy. I want to shout! He's got a bit of a smile on his face. I'm feeling good. Daddy doesn't talk a whole lot, but I think today he might see that I can work along with him and raise sheep with the best of them. Josie looks pretty good there, wearing her ribbon. We've got to stay now here in the barn so that people can take pictures and stuff and ask about how I raised Josie. Daddy is just outside the pen now.

"You did really good there, son…you'n Josie," he says, smiling at me. "Smile a little for the pictures."

I feel just a little bit taller.

"Yes sir. Thank you, Daddy."

GOLDFISH

I've always thought of my daughter as lucky. Maybe "blessed" is the proper description. You see, when she was baptized she was specially immersed, like Achilles, but she's been lucky. For instance, when she was a toddler and we would go to the store, I would give her lottery scratch cards to occupy her and she always came up a winner! She would usually get a small treat and then the rest would go in her bank. Her birthday is on ninth; some people consider that a lucky number. Once at Yankee Stadium after making friends with all the people in our section, a guy with his friends gave her the ball that came flying so close we had to duck. And then there were the goldfish.

Veronica must have been seven or eight when we went to one of the street fairs, most likely, an Italian Street Festa. We walked and ate treats and played some games, and there was the one where you'd win a pair of goldfish. Of course, she won! Great! At this time, we had already had a menagerie in the home, including her father's ever-multiplying tank of goldfish—all named Oscar, but in the course of separation, we got the dog and the hamster, everything else going to him. But now we also had fish.

I was a bystander to the caretaking of fish. My ex-husband was the expert. I had my own goldfish as a kid, but they never lasted very long. The ex came over and enthusiastically took care of his daughter's new pets. Setting up the goldfish bowl up with some nice gravel and a little mermaid statue, and in went the fish. Personally I couldn't understand why he went through this whole set-up other than he had all the supplies. I never knew *anyone* who had these street fair fish more than a week or two, including myself. Of course I was semi-responsible to overseeing the whole production. My ex said since it was two little goldfish, no need to clean the bowl more than every couple of weeks. He said he'd come by and clean it. Good! But I knew in reality that would not be the case.

Cleaning fish bowls and tanks is a disgusting job, and I wanted nothing to do with it. I had been witness to this before. It involves first removing the fish with some of their dirty water into another bowl or bucket, siphoning out the remaining water down the drain, and rinsing the gravel, best done in a colander of some sort, and the bowl. Also a good thing is to have a gallon jug of water standing by that's been aerating for a few days, rather than freshwater from the faucet. Then you put everything back together. Did I mention the Tetra-Fin food? The Super-Food of Fish. Just a pinch. My daughter was quite on point with that pinch of food, as her dad showed her.

And so the days and weeks passed, and then the months as well. Holy Cow! The fish were still alive! My ex, as I expected, at first was obliging in coming by pretty regularly and cleaning that bowl. Thank God! Then he started slacking, and I was given instructions to tend to the dirty bowl that looked gross and was starting to smell in my kitchen. Great! No way was I making this a regular activity. I was taking care of a child, taking care of a dog, a hamster, and now the fish because both the other parties had abdicated their care-taking roles. Dog crap, hamster crap, and now fish droppings—UGH! And then it was a year later. *Who* has fish from a street fair, in a plastic sandwich bag that lives a year?!

My lucky Veronica!! DAMN!

Well I'd had enough with the goldfish: the bowl was dirty, and… I "accidentally" overfed them. Too big a pinch for a few days. Oops! First one, then the other took that long ride down the sewer pipe to the Great River of Dead Goldfish. Fortunately Veronica accepted that these fish just don't live that long, and she was very lucky to have had them a year. Also I was fortunate that her dad backed me up on this, although he was a little surprised that they had died. They had been doing so well. Yeah…well, the bowl was very dirty. He offered replacements from his Oscar's feeder tank. That was an entire tank of goldfish for his big fishes. "No thank you," I said, "You can enjoy the fish when visiting your father." Our fish were not replaced. Lucky for me.

Peggy Liegel

No One Imagined

No one imagined the storm would be that bad—
Four at the table
Only three the next day,
The table floating away.

No one imagined the storm would be that severe—
The night the lights went out
And it stayed that way.

The burnt board with the nail and the color red
Ripped right through
Stuck on the sand-cemented beach.

It was a choice
To go to sleep or to wake up
After storm had passed.

Waking up, the fear going into it
After eyes see first
The nothing that is there.

I Felt Loved

I lied, forgiven
Or not forgiven.

Mad at me
Still was loved,
So he said,.

So very angry
Belt broke me.

Bleeding red raw
Still was loved,
So he said.

I was forgiven
Now he said.

Forgiven by him,
Healing took long.
Forgiving him, too,

I felt love.

LEAVE TAKING

Don't leave home without it. The little brown leather toiletry bag that belonged to my father comes to mind. Inside, the morals of youth all emptied out except for the smell of his aftershave.

His sandpaper chin against my cheek handing me a suitcase and a towel is our secret. How had he even guessed I was planning a clean break, a radical-forever-getaway? I'd had enough. He had too, but he'd already sunk his whole life down into this failed attempt at home and wouldn't or couldn't get back up.

He didn't want me to go away empty-handed; had nothing left to give except silent, defeated approval in a handed-over towel and suitcase that snapped shut this little bit of him, a clue: his toiletry bag placed inexplicably inside.

I left without saying thank you, choked by the searing embrace of stubbly chin on my soft cheek. Although barely touched, he had rubbed me raw. Met too scared of him to ever catch those rare, fleeting flashes of warm-brown in his pained-angry eyes.

I left with a mostly empty suitcase and no place to really go. The suitcase implied destination; I became a traveler. Inside a fold of the silk interior lining, he'd slipped two hundred dollar bills wrapped round and round a red velvet ribbon that I discovered the same night I'd owned the suitcase by opening and closing it over and over again, just to hear the snap, snap, snap, snap/snap, snap, snap.

The bright-orange suitcase was brand new, but the towel he'd given me wasn't. It was the dog's towel—well-worn, frayed at the edges; a soft-cotton terry turned dirty that I had wrapped the mutt in many a day when he'd come back wet and muddy from hunting varmints and limping a bit.

How could such a mean man, my papa, know the comfort I would receive in this old rag of a towel pressed against my teary, useless face two nights later in a faraway place, the night I first heard Handel's Messiah and travelled on "Comfort Ye, My People" holding on.

STANDING

As she walks the sidewalk sideways,
The cracks are felt beneath her shoes.
The growing fields ring round her still.
She picks apart the daisies bound to her,
White petals of love and love me (k)nots.
Unlucky and lucky in love, she lets their softness fall
And listens to her beating heart.

I hear resonating sounds of soil turned under
The Germanic guttural sounds.
Related killing related
The staggering der, die, das of
Commanded obedience,
The stubbornness in longer sentences—
The longing.

The ivory keys of black and white
Touch down and rise up,
Slapping roses onto cheeks—
Senseless thorns.

I hear sounds resonating.
The soil is being turned under and uprooted.

She carries her bucket of water
From grandmother's first memory of crossing the ocean
The blue that grew skyward and embraced newness
In all its confusion, clear.

She holds rocks as strength going right through her
As she grew through them.
These things the soil holds get picked through.
She collects and assigns them meaning

When soil is turned under and up righted.

She is willing to die and be reborn
But not like her sister
Have bronzed four-year-old shoes
Stick between the Virgin Mary blue.

She thinks through the power
    Of stillness
And struggles with forgiving
    That what she holds most dear
        IS LOVE

Is silence
Is touch
The feeling between words
Transmitted among people.

Soil being turned upright
    Parts this cyclical year.
The body unstuck is hers alone.

Freed grows different.
    Released from the soil
Stands upright

And moves closer to the unknown,
Leaving grandmothers with braids
S boat on the water
Bobbing through waves.

As fear in the belly
　　So round,
It's welcomed.
The families passed through her
Leaving strings that untangled
As a source of great strength
And there she is.
She is standing.
Riding in the Rewind of Fast Forward.
Riding in the rewind of fast forward IS
　　Opening up our windows of opportunity
　　　　And breathing deeply
There once was a storm I have yet to recover from
　　And I'm not sure why
I see the windows through which this happened over time
　　　　As once upon a time.
The shades are drawn in shadows deep.

The extreme weather caught me unaware.
What gave way was my mind.
I left it there and travelled on.
The scene is in literature, now a separate book.
The woman picks up and smiles.
I survived.
It is a happy ending.

But part of me didn't.
And I want to go back and get that, too
Before it storms again.

The scene is about going back to collect what broke.
The family at the grave, dancing down the soil
Attached an end date a name.
Three graves surrounding we three left...
The unresolved, time dissolving.
There are different windows with drawn shades.
This scene is about opening the blinds to see more clearly what
Remains.
The action takes place in winter in two places.
The resolution is healing; the story yet to be written.
There was a confusing problem:
I receive the script to the wrong play.
The obvious solution
Am returning to write parts one and two:
"The Winter Winds Blues" and
"When wind comes through closed windows."
Am getting my money back, a full refund.

I'll make money my own story
About functioning again
And loving again.
Perhaps 'tis a light-hearted comedy of falling water
That ends beside the ocean.
In the merry-go-round of dancing horses
I am riding Winter.
Autumn is behind me
And Spring ahead.
I

Susan Massad

Cancer II

We live in the age of cancer. I am of an age where cancer is a frequent visitor.

A long deep note held for six seconds. Three short notes—high pitch, six clangs, and then the recurring deep note. It is not "Nixon in China," although it could be mistaken for a John Adam's work. This jarring song of the MRI is heard in hospitals, clinics, and in shopping mall throughout the country. It is a tune that "we" the patients have become all too familiar. It is "Cancer in America," an MRI opera.

Cancer came unexpected this time around. Boom! Loudly and with pain. It was very different from the first bout four years ago. That was painless, a breast lump, low grade, and noninvasive. The lump was removed, followed by three weeks of radiation therapy, and then it was "all gone." It was not a big event in my life and not nothing. I had entered the ranks of one in eight US women who have a breast-cancer diagnosis and, by all criteria, could be considered a survivor.

Yesterday, my daughter asked me how I was, and my reply was "pretty good," although I had spent more times in tubes this week than I cared to, or could even imagine.

Blessed with a good, not really excellent, health for the first seventy-five years of my life, this abrupt and unanticipated thrust into the world of cancer treatment—regular monitoring, monthly treatments, and the "waiting for results" rituals—was jarring. It was an intrusion into my formerly "healthy" life.

The MRI sounds—clang, pause, dim, dum, dim dum, ring pause, clang, a veritable symphony—continued for an hour and a half as my spine was measured, pondered over by the magnetic rays, studied, with and without contrast, to ascertain whether healing taken place in the cancer invaded collapsed T9 vertebrae, or, more importantly, was there "new evidence" of spread?

"How are you? How are you feeling?" dilemma.

I have a wide circle of wonderful friends, many whom I have known and worked with for years. Some have been patients and friends over the course of my fifty-plus years of medical practice, and others date back to my high-school years. Since the breast cancer returned six months ago, I have been in medical mode. At times feeling well, out and about participating in all the offerings of an active and full life, and other times relatively housebound, tired, and limited in what I can do. Many friends call, write, and visit in person. They ask me, "How are you doing? How are you feeling?"

In the play *Wit* by Margaret Edison, Vivian Bearing, the lead character, points out the absurdity of the "How are you doing?" question when she is lying in a hospital bed, tubes connected to every orifice, vomiting uncontrollably, or simply known to be dying of metastatic ovarian cancer. I do not experience the "How are you doing?" questions as absurd, but rather I feel deeply the caring, the love, and the concern behind these questions. My inclination is to answer them honestly and share with my friends something of my experience. I want to be giving to them. The other me says no, no I do not want to give any more. Cancer is only one thing in my life, and I don't want to give this disease one more inch of space in my life. I want my non-sick, non-having-cancer life back.

I have committed my life to living socially, giving, and creative endeavors with other people whom I love and care about. They ask me "how are you doing" from a place of caring, and I am ever appreciative that I am not doing my cancer alone. When I am at my best, I can share with friends and family the frustration and difficulty of living my life day to day with cancer. Such expression always draws us closer.

In *Performance of a Lifetime*, my dear friend, the late Fred Newman, philosopher, therapist, and author, speaks about the medical model that gives a name to our distress/dis-ease and then proceeds to relate to us as who we are. In society we are cancer victims, and it is expected that we will conform to the idealized socially determined understanding of survivorship, cure, beating of the odds.

The MRI opera continues and finally ends with a long ringing sound. Exiting the tube, the always helpful technician takes my hand and says, "Times up." We perform this ritual together, leaving the stage to the next actor already dressed and prepped for his or her role. Having cancer is just one part of my life. I, as many with this seemingly overwhelming disease, struggle to give it the attention, and/or lack of attention, that it warrants at any particular time while we continue to live, performing our lives.

East 68th Street

Exiting the subway at East 68th and Lexington, I walk down the street with my friend David, a fifty-year-old African American man from the Bronx. We are going to visit a top-of-the-line cardiac surgeon at New York Cornell Weil Hospital Center, the crown jewel of an ever-expanding village of hospitals and clinics that are located at the foot of East 68th as it meets the East River. David has developed coronary artery disease and heart failure, a result of genes, a fat, rich diet, stress, and the many other risk factors that are endemic in our poor communities of color. We have been friends for over thirty years, working side by side to build a nonprofit organization that is home to a national network of performance-based programs dedicated to the growth and development of young people from our poorest communities. David now lives in Chicago, where he is a revered community youth leader. He has returned to New York City for this crucial visit to be with old friends who love and care for him. We are traveling to this prestigious hospital for a second opinion as to whether David needs open-heart surgery to unblock his clogged arteries.

As we walk east down 68th, I feel the familiar knot-in-the-stomach, heart-pounding, anxious anticipation from many years past that once accompanied me as I tore down from the subway to make it in time for early morning medical rounds. It was 1962. A newly minted physician, graduate of the University of California at San Francisco Medical Center, I had elected to leave the safety and warmth of

California family to begin a residency in New York City's notorious Bellevue Hospital. The hook that brought me east was a chance to live in the big city, work at one of its best-known municipal hospitals, and immerse myself in the blood-and-guts "real" world, front-line medicine for which Bellevue was famous.

I was disappointed that my first rotation as a real doctor was not at Bellevue but, rather a four-month stint at another hospital in the area of New York Cornell Weill Hospital. On the days I was not on call, I took the subway to work and would often be running down 68th Street, white coat flapping, always late, and anxious about what the day might bring.

Today this much-traveled street has been remodeled, reworked, and renovated as it moves into the ranks of a rich and fashionable Manhattan neighborhood. No longer lined by five-story walk-ups, delis on every corner where one could sit at a counter and have a chocolate egg cream, or toasted corn, with or without butter. Gone were the pocket playgrounds and street vendors.

We pass by a golden-yellow, forty-five-story Trump high-rise surrounded by beautifully attended urban gardens. Next, a solid block long, white tile fronted apartment building with a one story high, inflated rat signifying an active union dispute. Men in hard hats and glowing yellow vests give us leaflets as we pass by. Exquisitely renovated brownstones line the south-side of the block between Lexington and 2nd Avenue—every detail done to perfection. Sounds of pounding, roadwork, jackhammers, and the construction of the 2nd Avenue subway, disharmonious, and shrill, defy efforts to maintain the studied decorum of this now fashionable neighborhood.

In 1962 I was young, naïve, loved the work of being a doctor, and, was in those pre-women's movement days, mostly oblivious to the sexism, authoritarianism, inequities, and injustices of our training system. The ratio of women to men was one to ten; the chief resident, always a man, dictated our rotations and hours of work. We were on call every other night, and for those twenty-four-hour stretches considered ourselves lucky if we managed to capture one to two hours of sleep. Call on the weekend was for a full forty-eight hours. This is what we had signed up for. There was no Bell Commission or doctors' union to regulate our hours and/or quality of work. You pushed patients to X-ray, sat up with them all night when they were unstable, and often were the one carrying the blood work to the laboratory five blocks away. The complaining we did was a mix of braggadocio and compassion. "I got three hours of sleep last night; how about you? The nurse called me every hour for an order! She is a killer. That's really rough. We had six admissions back-to-back on 4W; how did you do?"

Morning rounds during that first rotation started precisely at eight. For rounds you were expected to be on time, reasonably well groomed, prepared to present your new cases in detail, and take part in a discussion of the fine points of your patient's care no matter what the night before had yielded in the way of sleep. Coffee, adrenaline, and, in those days before the Surgeon General's report, cigarettes kept us going. The chief of medicine, Cunningham, was bald, rotund, and a leader in his field. Kindness, compassion, and empathy were not yet valued attributes of this doctor, or, in fact, for most doctors, at that time. It was all about knowing—knowing a lot, knowing more than others, letting others know how much you know, and letting innocents like us know that we did not know anything all. Cunningham was also a roué. He made suggestive comments to the nurses, told "off-color jokes" on rounds, and was legendary for peeing in the sink in his office no matter who was present. We, the most junior of residents, were in awe and completely intimidated.

The food was good and free, available at all hours in the canteen. The patients were sick, scared, often in pain, and, in those days before

Elizabeth Kubler Ross took up the cause of the rights of the dying, were never, ever told they had a cancer diagnosis.

Bedside rounds that followed the morning rounds with "the boss" were my favorite—talking to patients, offering what comfort we could, planning therapies, and ongoing care. The deception that everyone was in the hospital bed for an alternative illness, a set-back, a special treatment for a growth, maybe a tumor but never cancer, was painful and always in the room. We worked hard, did our best, and, in moments of time-out, indulged in macabre jokes about cancer, our patients, and the idiosyncrasies of the various attending doctors whom we worked with.

The New York style of medicine was aggressive, male in all its attributes, rough and tumble, and very foreign to me coming from the more laid-back, although always sexist, slightly more genteel atmosphere of my California medical school. I had been an exemplary student and had my pick of hospitals for postgraduate training. I had chosen Bellevue. My strengths were in good patient care. I was not a knower, or rather I was not very good at letting others know how much I knew.

It was a huge shock to be told four months into my first year that I was going to be cut from the program the following year. There would be no job for me. The peeing-in-the- sink-doctor did not recommend me. The form of graduate medicine then was a pyramid system that required one-fourth of the class be dropped at the end of the first year. There was no recourse or redress if one felt these decisions were unjust. That is just the way it was. I was very humiliated. In my short twenty-four years of life, I had never experienced that kind of failure.

In the end I did not leave the program. The Vietnam War was heating up and a third of my fellow trainees were tapped for the doctor's draft. They needed me. The program, not so humbly, asked me if I would consider being part of their second-year program. I accepted rather than make the life change that moving to a new hospital in a new location required. This episode in my life was painful. I was growing up, learning something about how the world worked and how to navigate the very competitive, sexist, and technologically driven, often inhumane, world of medicine.

David and I arrive at NY Hospital right on time. We walk thru the cavernous, elegantly appointed marble lobby and travel up to the fourth floor where we meet with the chief of cardiac surgery. He is courteous, matter of fact, very direct about what he can offer David to repair his damaged coronary arteries, and respectfully answers our most pressing questions. It is not an intimate conversation but a very good consultation. We leave with sufficient information to work with, and to make a decision.

I have wanted to be a doctor since I was very young. For the most part, in my fifty-plus years of medical practice, I looked forward to going to work everyday. My relationship with my chosen profession, so flawed and difficult in many ways, has always been conflicted. As David and I travel up 68th Street, we talk, laugh, and make a plan to have the surgery. Conflicts and all, I am so grateful that we have a medicine that can benefit my deserving and dear friend David.

Michelle McCartney

Could Try Harder

Oh! Lord
Let it be OK for me to be sick,
To have cancer
To not have to be "fine" all the time.

It's finished, over I think. I see you whisper.
Time to move on.

When I falter do not think me selfish.
A sigh does not mean I've given up,
Or, that I insist on the centre stage.
Tiredness is a reality not a ploy.
Do not be afraid for you or for me, for
Sometimes all I want to do is
Cry. Not die. Just cry.

The old me has departed, so that the new could be born
Even if she doesn't suit, or allay your fears
Of my mortality or of your own.
She's here.

So I point my gun at the head of guilt
And the heart of hopelessness, for
I have rubbed me out—not all of me—and
Here is to the re-drawing!

For I have but two options:
A happy long life
Or a happy short life. It's nonnegotiable.

Join me on this stage. There are plenty of parts for all.
But please do not take offense
When I say, that this time I choose
To write the script myself.

And NO, today I do *not* feel fine!
And that's OK, too.
But thanks for caring.

A Bird's Song

Don't talk to me about nature and bird's singing and all that malarkey. I'm one of these poor unfortunates who love the sedentary life. That is what windows are for, isn't it?—for looking out of! There is nothing like a miserable wet day by a big roaring fire with none of that guilt that I should be out there expanding my lungs and other parts of my anatomy. However, lately, something has changed in my philosophy—me. My physical shape is no longer embracing my cerebral lifestyle.

I've noticed that my waist is disappearing at an alarming rate, and I am beginning to look like a sack of potatoes with a belt tied around it. I've read *that* book—you know the one—"10 Days to a Flatter Stomach"! Well, I've come to the opinion that that happy state won't be achieved by just reading it! So, to avoid having to cut out too much food, I've decided to take the bull by the horns and launch myself outside to discover the joys of nature and that's when the craic really started!

To begin this crusade into health and "oneness with nature," it is necessary to embark upon the rather awesome task of finding a nice quiet country road to amble along! Not an easy task these days. And so I stepped out on to the main road in front of our country house. Right away my senses are assaulted by a massive juggernaut hurtling down the road with hundreds of tree trunks on the back of it, propelled by a driver that looks like one of those Rockie Mountain lumberjacks. And of course, just when he's level with me, those air brakes let out that dreadful hissing sound that is similar, I'd imagine, to the sound of a giant with flatulence!

Follow this with a boy racer, in a souped—up Escort, complete with spoilers and noisy exhaust, careering along. From his car radio I hear that "thump" "thump" noise that would be what a headache would sound like if it had a noise. Now either that young man drives past our house very often or all those aspiring Formula 1 drivers are listening to the same song.

But, I'm actually out of the house now, and I won't be deterred by such vehicular aberrations. And so I press on. After an arduous ascent, I make it up a steep brae, and by now my calf muscles are stretched painfully like taut elastic just about to snap. My chest is beginning to feel like it has turned to lead. At last I reach a side road that is wonderfully flat and tranquil, or so I hope.

It is a lovely spring morning. Everything seems so fresh and clean. The hedgerows are a tapestry woven with shades of translucent green. I sigh and allow my eye to rove across a landscape of willow, blackthorn hedges and small, fertile fields. The birds vie for airspace, and each note seems so shrill and clear.

Yes, I am beginning to feel that I can really breathe—as if I have been let out of a lift trapped on the twentieth floor of the Empire State building. Lambs skip and frolic, reminding me that it will soon be Easter. Darn it—there I am thinking of food again.

And then I remember that there used to be a dump on this road. I think of all those more persistent rodents that might have decided not to move habitat upon its closure. Having a very active imagination, I envision pairs of beady eyes watching me from thickets on luxuriously verdant banks as I pass along singing at the top of my voice in the vain hope of piercing their eardrums and thus encouraging them to relocate elsewhere. My mind is racing and so is my blood pressure as it makes steady upward progress.

Then, as if things weren't bad enough, two nasty-looking farm dogs come racing down a lane. Sweet divine mercy! Now I am on the verge of tears. Next time I'll carry a brick in my designer handbag! I remember a neighboring farmer and how he used to roar at his dog in a terribly gruff way, and so in desperation I try some of the same. As I hunch down to get on "all fours," I let out a howl that has never been emitted from my vocal chords before, and, begorra, it works! Off the dogs go with their tails between their legs, and I, now feeling that wee bit braver, stick my tongue out at their retreating backsides. I have to retrieve it quickly as a farmer trundles along on a Ferguson T20 and spots my undignified pose. I smile weakly and scurry along.

Not long until Joan's house now. A half a mile, I'd say. She lives up this long lane that boasts an impressive number of potholes of all shapes and sizes. It suddenly occurs to me that the road leading up to the lane is deserted and that there is neither a dwelling nor sign of humanity to be seen.

My pace begins to quicken in tandem with my heartbeat. I now begin to wish that I wasn't ideologically opposed to mobile phones. Anything could happen to me out here, and, as all my friends know of my aversion to exercise, it will never occur to anyone that I have gone for a walk! I can see it now the headlines in the tabloids (or at least the local *Sentinel*) "Would-be Author Vanishes." Heh! maybe I'll become famous postpartum or is it postmortem? I hope they can find that memory stick I lost last month. There were some mighty writing pieces on that!

I turn a corner and, mercifully, I finally see my destination. As I reach the half door, the delicious waft of a decent Ulster fry-up envelopes my now depleted body. Talk about a wonderful sensual experience! The perilous journey is at an end. I've survived! My old mate and I do what we do best and blether on for hours. Just when it gets to the time for me to retrace my weary steps, a wondrous thing occurs, proving without a doubt that there is a God—the sky opens and the rain buckets down in absolute torrents. Joan, bless her, insists on running me home. I accept her kind offer for who am I to hurt her feelings for the sake of a few calories burned?

For My Son, Jim

It isn't easy
I know.
But I ask you to believe
When despair seems to have invaded your life
Again.
But pray, believe,
That hope will float
Up through the mire that
Is your sorrow
So that you will
One day smile
Like you never smiled before
Laugh 'til your temples are taut as
Knicker elastic in a homemade slingshot
And that you will
Love like your heart
Is made of giant marshmallows.

Is it selfish of me to ask, to beg of you
To Believe?
But I do.
Because…because,
Well, just because,
I love you.

THE DAFFODIL

I was feeling low, so low,
When I found her,
Under a log.

There she was, no single drop of sunshine
Had kissed her limbs from birth.
But she lay there, almost perfect in form
But for the fact that she was yellow-stemmed.
As yellow as the flower she was trying to be.
My heart leapt, jump-started from its sluggish grief
To see her prostrate, needing but not needy.

Within my distant soul, I felt it grow,
The miracle that is of Spring and hope.
I found myself prising her out gently, lovingly
To lodge her among her peers.

She looked curiously proud, of her difference.

And why not.
That little crittur' who didn't know how to,
Not want to go on.

Jack Robert Nix

Quittant la Maison
(Leaving Home)
March 2016

ROOM

I am walked to the room.

surprised by its size.
like the gardens at giverny
much smaller than expected.

not nearly as nice
not even nice
downright awful.
giverny is indignant.

nurse: everything off. gown on table.

I do as I am told.
strip bare
cover with gown
wear socks
wait.

the room is cold and sterile
but feels dirty.
the lighting hurts my skin
or maybe it is the room.

dr. urologist enters
he has an appealing manner.

it does not compensate.
his manner, that is

for the room
or the lighting

or the gown
or what is going to happen.

the area is numbed
a needle passes through my rectum.

I see nothing
I feel nothing

just the sound of the needle extracting bits of tissue
it is the sound of a staple gun.

it pops twenty-four times.

I know
I count

I am a specimen.

WAITING

the room is blanketed in bad carpeting.
wall to wall and easy to clean.
it seems like an efficient place.
filled with people
who only live today.

it has been an hour, and with the october chill,
the one preceding winter – I am stooped, old and dry.
except I am not. dry.
I am wet. with sweat. cold.
becoming. old.

she leads me to the room.
where he did the biopsy.
now only me. alone in the cold.
it still has a dirty sterile attitude.
like an old whore who doesn't give a shit.

I watch him approach.
he wears the same white coat uniform.
now only five steps away.
I concentrate on his face.
what can I discern.

nothing.

not an acquittal.
not a conviction.
just a lazy jury.

it has been a week.
    the results are not back.
        it feels cruel.
        a mean joke.

he is a nice man.
a kind who wants to be liked.
    he spins it for me.
    bad results bring fast returns.
like losing in a landslide.
but good results bring slow returns.
    like fine wine. slow to age.

I leave as a glass of merlot.
    still walking with a stoop.
        feeling old not aged.

RESULTS

I was a lazy. uninterested. student.
   really not my thing. inhibiting. and confining.
I liked pass/fail. "p/f."
   figure out minimum effort.
and you got a "p."
   off just a little.
and you got an "f."

I was never off. close.

biopsy results are similar.
   positive/negative. except more.
grades are included.
   as if you scored a "pass" and in the report they buried a "d."

someone named gleason grades prostate cancer biopsies.
   1-10.
I scored a 9.
   that is bad.
in school high grades are good.

this takes getting used to.
   negative=good. positive=bad.
   low score=good. high score=bad.
it has to do with differentiation between the good and bad.
the greater the difference.

the higher the grade. the more aggressive
    the.
    it.

dr. urologist is explaining as dennis takes notes.
        I stare.
    good.bad.positive.negative.pass.fail.
        g.b.p.n.p.f.
    I..a.m..n.u.m.b.

he talks options.
    surgery.
    radiation.
both.
    act quickly.

he hands me report. my card. "f/p/9." failed/positive/9.

    will I be expelled

FILLETED

jackie insisted on accompanying me.
to hospital.
   god awful mourning hour.
   that is kind.
we sat in somewhere.
I was called. into surgery.
   the chamber looked like a shiny new kitchen.
   stainless steel around.

count backwards from 10.

that was it.
I am not awake. then. I am.
   my head beats.
   I hear. a woman's voice.

…repeating…repeating…repeating…..

"I am always attracted to unavailables."

did I die.
and transcend to the land of self-pitying clichés.
she keeps talking.
   please shut up.
I can't speak.

then. I see.
joan and liz and henry.

liz flew down from boston. to be with joan.
    that is kind.
joan, who faints at sight of blood. is here. true to her word.
    that is kind.
drugs make me happy. even to see henry.
    that is kind.

moved to recovery.
others recovering.
    too.
it is night.
roberto visits.
he leans over bed railing. and kisses me.
    that is kind.

with sunrise it hurts.
    I become a vampire.
    it really hurts.
I have been kicked.
by something.
    not human.

it. is not. kind.

APOLOGIES

surgery was easy. in hindsight. 3 months later. I feel fine. stopped
peeing myself, too.
add that to kind.

then another apologetic dr call.
dr surgeon: "I am sorry, …"

      I know the rest.

is there anything worse. I don't want them happy. delivering news. of
my possible demise. but apologize. come on. can't we come up with
something more creative. what was all that education for. dammit.
      anger, missy.
how to respond:

if-then-else program.

if dr. apologetic
    then
        I grow apoplectic
    else
go to high road.

high road.

if high road
    then

I say
> "you are forgiven' or "no problem" or "don't be silly" or
> "oh, that's ridiculous"

else
> go to gracious.

gracious.

if gracious
> then
> > I say
> > > "thank you"

I go to gracious

and am sucked up. in a cloud. and rained down. in a sea. it is vast. uncomprehendingly dark. I am alone. I kick off my shoes. I try to float. don't fight the waves. you will tire. it brushes against me. here. by myself. in the middle of the sea. in the lightless black. fright infuses my movement. I begin to swim. panic swimming. against the waves. toward nothing. and lose my breath.

> lucy: "ethel! ethel! help me hide this elephant. before ricky finds out!"

how do. I. not find out.

ETC.

from: dr. surgeon
to: me
subject: next step
action: wait & see

I don't like the sea. I don't like what i don't see. and I don't see the
sea. as you see.

I don't wait. I don't sea. I flee.

I am behind the wheel.
   let go and let god.
      does he have a license.

god never gives you more than you can bear.
   oh really, miss platitudes.
      ever talk to a dead person.

and. just in case. you did not no. talk is miserly.
   the passenger seat is free. care to join. me.

where did she go.

is frantic the same as scared.
   or more like terror.
the story has veered off narrative.
into oncoming.

I need to get out of this lane.
my hands grip the wheel.
it won't move.

I blink.
it crashes. through glass.

    and strikes.
    across dashboard. my arm.

it smiles.
I freeze.
it drags.
    me.
    over concrete highway.

asphalt keens.

HE IS:

from: me
to: dr. radiation
subject: I am breaking
action: help. please.

from: dr. radiation
to: me
subject: next next step
action: fight

he is strong. he is invincible. he is:

no. wrong song.

I feel like marlene dietrich introducing burt bacharach.

he is:

my arranger. my accompanist. my conductor.

he is:

dr. radiation. my general.

I sign up. 8-weeks-boot-camp. 5-days-per-week. every-week. for
8-weeks.
each week more weak.

I am a soldier. I even get tattooed. it is for the bullets. electron.
high beam. but I dislike the uniform. a hospital gown. the barracks
fill. with other soldiers. and their visitors. the gown does not fit my
script. not that it is not. red carpet ready. it is not. but I am not

really sick. can I pretend. to be a visits. this way no one has to know.
I don't...

then it's over.

I wait. results. win. lose. battle. war.

phone hisses.

I am pleading. on my knees. begging.

it is. my last chance. to kill. it.

dad: if you shoot someone. kill him. or she will be back.
             to kill you

dr. radiation: I am sorry...

sound: gunshots

walter neff: goodbye, baby

cue: cry

I can't.

NEW STRATEGY

dr. radiation.
　　he is contrite.

I feel I should comfort him. but I have lost my comfort.
it has been torn away. or torn asunder. maybe rent asunder.

o.k. I am swerving into oncoming clichés.

ricky: "lucy, mira que tiene cosa..."

yes. I am numb. the world is my sterile. dirty. exam room. what.
to. do. I know. I will not feel. yes. that is it. make mom proud. no
muss. no fuss. do not feel. and I will not. humiliate you. that is
what feeling gets. and it does. get you. but then. what are feelings
for. shut up

　　wish to numb = call henry

what .. you .. are sick .. whaaat. he stretches out the words. it is im-
possible he forgot. he cannot be that stupid. he is playing. of course.
pretending not to know. really. no. in time I learn. he really does
not care. I mean seriously not. I move him from lousy friend box. to
shitty human being box. no offense meant. to shitty humans.

　　anger, missy

at least I got not to feel.

I am given names of 3 genitourinary oncologists. you must. see them. now.

one in each major hospital.

monty hall arrives.

me:	I thought you were dead
monty:	I am. now pick one
me:	pick what
monty:	a door dummy
me:	I can't
monty:	all right. I will show you what is behind each door
monty:	door number one
announcer:	dr glacé. empathy deficient. scary at bedside. otherwise brilliant
me:	next
monty:	door number two
announcer:	dr lumière. interesting. attractive. witty. intelligent. articulate
me:	but wtf he just say
monty:	door number three
announcer:	dr charismé. also medical reporter. direct. but nice. for network evening news
me:	would I get to meet david muir
monty:	grow up
me:	please
monty:	pick one

DOOR NUMBER TWO

I choose door number two. dr cornell. he is very smart. articulate.
does not rush me.
add him to kind. I just wish I understood what he was saying. what
the hell was that.

de niro: you talkin to me

I can not listen. but I do. he lays it out. I can not hear.

it is not something we play with. you mean like taking it to the park.

he is not fooling. he wants to totally oppress it. shut it down. yeah.
let's go for it.
what are we shutting down.

oh. that's what you had in mind. well. I have to think it over. what
happens if we don't.
like totally oppress it.

you will die
        say again
            you heard me

treatment starts. daily pills two weeks before special-L. side effects
are manageable.
yeah, so long as you're not the one managing. pills cause headaches.
eyes light sensitive.
I begin wearing sunglasses. even indoors. I am too old for attitude.

special-L causes sun-partched-desert-trekking fatigue. and impoten-
cy, too.
like surgery and radiation don't. additionally, it crushes your libido.
say what!

o.k. o.k. think. think hard. think harder. think hardest.

did he say manageable
    I believe he said die, sir
        thank you, carson

hmm...
    ruins performance. not to fret. strangles desire. too.

        every cloud has a tin plated ...

get my agent on the phone. now! yes. that's right. at the very least.
    I better get a silver-lined-cloud nomination out of this.
        I don't care. make it happen.

and while I have you. where's my oscar. susan hayward won one.
    very similar role. she wore high heels. walking to gas chamber.
        I am much better!

I still don't care. make it...did she hang up.

I could use a drink. hey. everyone. drinks on me.

    garbo: give me a whiskey. ginger ale on the side. and don't be
    stingy, baby

when did she start talking.

VEGAS

the casino is big. I am lost in its circles.

I lose money. playing poker. and stumble upon the roulette table. not russian. no guns.
play a few games. lose more money. why not. I head over to blackjack.

casino: I am sorry, sir. you are out of cash. credit. too.
me: but how
casino: I am sorry, sir

 those words.

I lose my feet. at least I do not see them. but. it does not stop me. from walking.

I lose my suite. and clothes. it doesn't matter. no one notices. across the street.
people I know. there. right there. who. no. I thought I did.

the strip looks small. tall casinos create delusions. I will walk the length.
what else can I do. if I am to see the other side. I wish to see tigers. and white lions.
and bears who cling.

 no veda. not oz. siegfried & roy.

I wish to lie down with them. and the pyramids. in grade school we studied pyramids. john's mom, elsie, helped me build one. from clay. I pass sands and flamingos. there is venice. built into a casino.

very smart. it won't sink. across the way are fountains. filled with powders of gold. during timed intervals the fountains exhale. the powders dance and lift up, glancing a cloud, grayish white and filled with stars.

somewhere I put on red shoes. I want to rest in the fountains. the shoes won't come off.

dammit veda. not dorothy. victoria page.

I see elsie. she is part of the fountain. gold powder. I want her to know she introduced me to kind. but the red shoes will not let me. stop. then it stops. the fountains. cloud and streams of powder fade.

I want to stop.
just for breath.

but, the shoes keep moving.

I grow bedraggled.
and exhausted.

but, the shoes keep moving.

DENOUEMENT

disheveled and raw,
I am becoming pieces

of blight, dust strewn
across some unknown field.

time falls, like
scaffolding in collapse.

orphaned by the future,
I am fostered by the past.

in despair, my determination strengthens,
and bones stiffen in weaves of threaded steel.

now, with quick pursuit - and infanticidal intent, I find
my monstrous progeny staring its hollowed gaze.

reaching, with arms strained in fright,
I lift my mutating seed

resting head on my breast,
placing bottle to its lips.

silently,

I begin nursing, with milk,
infused by death's dissolution.

speechless,

it
pauses.

hesitantly,

I
begin.

circling planets
wrought fragile in tears.

‿❧

thank you, Dr.s.T. & Dr.a.S

‿❧

Juan Pagan

THE RIVER

IT'S A BRIGHT, SUNNY, QUIET morning in late August, and the two
are cuddled, sitting on a bench near the local high school, in front of
a river with orange and yellow kayaks going upstream that seem to
disappear the further they went up as they blended in with the early
autumn's trees yellow, gold, and light brown. The river's quiet flow
and soft bubbling by the edge of the bank had a way of soothing the
pain of any anxiety that could ever exist—a perfect kind of quiet with
a healing effect that no human-made medicine could ever achieve.

Margarita and Michael had a friendship since grade school that turned into a deep-rooted love for one another; with a realization within their hearts that they were meant for each other in spite of past, painful relationships, they decided to move forward and share a life together as one. Both went to the same high school and were very athletic. He was on the high-school soccer team and she on the swimming team. Michael, not so tall, is well built with a notably excellent posture; his humbleness was even more notable. Margarita, nearly the same height as Michael, is slender and solid, with a figure from which Barbie dolls were created. Just by looking at them, one can tell they were meant for each other. And if one could look into their hearts, there would be no doubt whatsoever they belonged one to the other. But she is very ill and he doesn't know.

Margarita tries to solve the problem of their eventual loss by just living life as happily as she can, sharing and giving that happiness to Michael. She plays music on her record player with messages of undying love and memories that last forever, while keeping him blind to the reality of her fate.

The evening is cool and breezy; she insists on a walk to the park near their old high school, by the river. "But sweetheart, it's almost midnight," Michael softly exclaims.

Once there, at the moment they step on to the park's open field, with both hands she grasps Michael around the back of his neck, presses her lips against his, and gives him a long, luscious kiss that leaves him out of breath. And then quickly releases him and runs into the field and shouts, "Catch me!"

Michael, smiling with dizziness—as if awakening from dream—was up for a challenge. Despite his excellent physique and toned muscles, this slender girl, this solid swimmer, and the love of his life could outrun him

On this occasion he caught her; only because she let him. They embraced sealing out the cool breeze in between them as they sealed in the warmth of their bodies to become one...

"Let's go by the river..." Margarita tells him.

And they went and sat by the river together. They shared their warmth and stared out into the water that glistened with reflections from lamp posts and lights from homes across the river. The river's quiet flow always had a way of soothing her anxieties away.

Michael, although immensely enjoying Margarita's spirited outbursts of love and affection, believes that Margarita is deliberately avoiding talking of plans for their future together. He thinks she's become childish living for the moment, and every time he gets lovingly firm and serious to discuss their future plans, she puts on a song on the record player—the same song each time—and sings along with it.

"Hey, come on honey, sweetheart..." Michael says softly to Margarita, trying hard not to interrupt her as she loses herself in a lyric. "Let' talk and make our plans for our future..."

"I am," she responds. "I am making plans for our future; and I have a secret; the secret is in this song."

Michael, feeling a bit bewildered, felt a sense of relief. And with the belief that that they have their whole life ahead of them to be together and start their family, he begins to sing along with Margarita and takes over the song as he sings his favorite lyrics:

If I could make days last forever, if words could make wishes come true.

I'd save every day like a treasure and then, again, I would spend them with you.

And then Margarita would take over the song and sing her favorite lyrics:

But there never seems to be enough time to do the things you want to do. If I had a box just for wishes...

And as the song played, they'd fall in love with each other again; every day they fell in love with each other again...and again...until...

Michael stands in a hospital room by Margarita's bedside holding her hand.

"Leaving this earth while being so in love with you," Margarita tells him, "and falling in love with you again as I am at this moment...I can only feel joy in my heart. I don't feel the pain all I feel is our love."

Michael was grieving, confused, and angry; he could not understand her sense of joy, her peaceful smile. Sensing his pain and confusion, she tells him, "The secret is in the song."

Months have gone by since Margarita passed. Michael finally had the strength to play their favorite song on her record player. He listened and carefully waited to hear the lyrics about the box; and he heard them, but this time with more clarity and revelation than ever before:

If I had a box just for wishes, and dreams that had never come true; the box would be empty except for the memory of how they were answered by you.

"I got it! I got it!" Michael exclaimed, as he looked up toward the window smiling with tears in his eyes. "I got it, Margarita! I got it!"

Michael rushed to the window, opened it, and looked out into the sky smiling. He then took the little record player to the windowsill, placed the record, and began to play their song. As the guitar softly plays the introduction, he looks up to the sky, "This is for you, Margarita."

As the song ends and the guitar strikes its final cord, again, he looks up to the sky and says, "Good-bye Margarita. Good-bye."

It's late April, a gorgeous day, and the cool brisk air seems to be giving in to the warmth of the bright sun.

Michael is cleaning out the apartment they shared; he's leaving town, moving. As he is cleaning, under the old record player and a bunch of other stuff he kept in a closet for Margarita, he finds a small box. Squinting with childlike curiosity, he wondered what was in the box and opened it.

"Oh, it's your father's things!" he said aloud. In the box was her father's old high-school ring; a black-and-white wedding photo of her mom and dad; vacation photos of them when she was a child—in one he's holding her up to a tree as she reaches for an avocado, and it made Michael smile to see her as a cute little kid—military dog tags when her father served in the war; and a purple heart. Michael remembered being at her father's burial, and all the pain Margarita suffered, and how he thought he would never be able to console her. But somehow she found peace and was able to accept the loss of her father.

Michael continues searching, and at the bottom of the box was a folded piece of paper; it had many creases: a page with lines, neatly ripped from a journal. It was a letter handwritten in script. It was dated April 12, and the year it was written, Michael realizes, Margarita must have been seven years old.

With the letter in hand, Michael leans toward the window for the light of the sun and begins to read aloud: *It's a very nice day today. The trees are beginning to bud and there is a certain beauty that cannot compare to when the trees are in full bloom. Perhaps it is the sense of a new beginning and the good feeling it instills within my soul. And it reminds me of the times when you and I, early in the morning, are looking out the window through the leafless trees watching the boats pass by the East River. And then I tell you that one day we will be looking through this window, but we will not be able to see the river—and then I ask you, "Why do you think we will not be able to see the river?" And I watch the cute little expression on your face as you ponder. And you answer, "At night, daddy, when it gets dark we can't see the river." "Very good," I say to you. "But there's another reason." And I begin to explain: "One day the trees will be in full bloom and no matter how hard we look through the window, we will not see the river. But we know it's there because we've seen it—and it will always be there. And one day the season will arrive when the leaves will fall and you will be able to see the river again... And just as the seasons arrive in perfect synchronized timing—as when the snow melts and the trees and flowers blossom and the leaves change color and begin to fall...so will the season arrive in which I will no longer be able to lift you up...or be there...but my love for you—just like the river—will always be there.*

CHILDREN WITHOUT LOVE

Holding me against my will and against the fence of the schoolyard, he jabs the barrel of a pistol into my mouth. The members of his gang laugh as he squeezes the trigger several times. They release me. Weak, helpless, crying, and outnumbered, I fall to the ground on hands and knees coughing, spitting, trying not to vomit. The weight of my small, frail body pressing the palms of my hands against the gritty cement ground causes pain as I push myself up. Several yards away, I see Rosa looking at me with such a pretty face and pitiful eyes desiring to help me. She is afraid, too, but the gaze upon her beautiful face comforts me.

He reloads his pistol at the gutter that boasts a stagnant puddle of murky, soiled water. He reenters the yard and now begins to prey on female victims. As he crouches behind each of his victims, he sticks the pistol under her skirt, pointing up, squeezing off as many shots as he can before his unsuspecting victim runs away in disbelief and disgust. He laughs in concert with his apostles of torment each time he accomplishes his demonic deeds.

Hot, sweating, and sunny, we are in the yard. Lunch recess at Public School 15 on the Lower East Side is in progress once again. He is coming again with his malicious misfits. My heart is crying and pounding as I look for Mrs. Gold or Miss Epstein. They are not about, and the pang in my heart becomes an almost cardiac arrest as he approaches me. He puts his hands on my shoulders, pressing down on me with Spock's Vulcan grips, hovering over me with his large, plump, chunky body as my heart pounds in my stomach, practically causing an unwanted bowel movement. He is staring into my face with his chunky, remorseless eyes sunk into his firm, puffy cheeks like a squinting hamster overstocked with food, smiling diabolically, as one of his misfits calls to him, "Over here." He pushes me, forcing me to walk backward, guiding me toward the voices of his demonic followers, "Over here, over here." We arrive.

Without warning, he shoves me to the cement ground, and painfully I land on my butt. An explosion of laughter bursts from his henchmen. He steps back, and standing like a hero, reigning over his bold deed, he smiles at me. His crew is laughing wildly. The pain on my butt bone is slowly subsiding as I begin to stand. Sensing something awry, I instinctively rub my hand across my behind and inadvertently scoop off the soft, warm, gooey excrement left behind by a dog. Its foul, repugnant odor makes me vomit the little I had for lunch, igniting another explosion of laughter.

He thought himself all-powerful and would not do the deed himself. He barks out an order for a volunteer. One steps forward.

"Can you kick his ass?" says Julio.

"Yeah, he's a chump," says his henchman.

"Go ahead," Julio says smiling.

Julio grabs me by the back of my collar, holding me to facilitate the blows of the volunteer. I brace for the impact when suddenly I hear the commanding, high-pitched voice of Miss Epstein yelling, "Julio, Julio..." She is running as fast as any sweet old lady can.

Running, running, now I am running, defying traffic lights and cars and the school-crossing guard, who is yelling, "Stop, stop," brushing my bloody nose against strange adults in my path—the lady carrying groceries who lives below me and the superintendent mopping the lobby of the old tenement, who calls out to me in his native tongue, "Juan, Juan, que te paso?"

I burst open the door of my home. I enter the kitchen and in blind anger grab a knife from the counter, knocking the pots and dishes to the floor. Running, running, I am running in blind rage back toward the door, frantically screaming, "I'm going to kill him. I'm going to kill him." In my furious haste I bump and bounce off a large, round belly of a soft, beautiful giant. Through my blurry, tear-filled vision I see the stern but sweet, bulldog face of my greatest defender.

Mama was a large woman with soft, pillow arms to wrap around me. I buried my face in her large breasts and tasted my own blood, mucous, and tears. Her large, soft belly wrapped in a moist smock with the fragrance of cooking grease and freshly washed dishes warms me, lifting me out of my pain, as has happened many times before. She speaks to me in her native tongue, "Dios esta contigo, mi hijo, Dios esta contigo" ("God is with you, my son. God is with you"). "Oh, no, He's not," I answer softly, but defiantly. "He is with you," she says. The mesmerizing effects of her embrace soothe my burning, racing heart, calming my anger. At that moment, God is with me. But where was He when I was in the schoolyard?

Connie Perry

Diagnosis

Apparently carcinoma is not the title of a song or of an anthology album by the famed Rock group The Cars. Imagine all their hits recorded from a place on tour back in the 1980s Cars in Noma.

And apparently it is not a Spanish or Portuguese or a foreign work for no way, no f'n way. Although that is entirely appropriate.

So, of course I am immediately on a tangent away from the concise definition of the words found on my lab results. Of course I am still in denial, thinking it is all just a cruel joke.

With a wicked punch line.

I got home from performing a stand-up comedy show, after a summer of getting back to the stage, after a summer of tests and more tests.

I got my lab results and referral instructions from my gynecologist in the mail.

There in black ink on white paper read endometrial carcinoma. That's in the lining of my uterus.

No f'in way.

So apparently endometrial is not the title of a landmark court case by a famed attorney general of anywhere. Imagine endome did something wrong, really really terribly wrong.

Although that is entirely appropriate.

So of course you see that I seek another tangent away from the concise definition of the words found on my lab results.

I'm still in denial.

THE STORY OF...

The story of my artistic and creative endeavors is like an amaryllis, a small miracle of flowering bulbs, that, when in bloom, transforms my soul.

It is elementary school, maybe sixth grade, and I was not content to follow the rules of that art class, which is to draw a friggin' still life. You know, items are arranged in a tableau—a vase, a glass, a stuffed squirrel, a candle, two eggs—all resting on a piece of velvet. We were to use pastels to draw what we saw but I was bored with the dull presentation of it all.

I needed to germinate my own originality. Plant the seeds of my own creativity. I needed to draw what I saw, an abstract and original view of things. I needed to master the medium of pastels in my own way by playing with the medium and smudging the colors, striking the paper and weeding through the process of new creativity.

In the end, I created the still life the teacher expected but in the back of my eleven-year-old mind I was raising the question "Who wanted to be like everyone else and mirror what had already been done?" Not I.

So I vaulted forward into my own plane of vision, hearing only my own tune—like playing bagpipes when everyone else was at a piano, striking forward on my own note, taking a risk, blowing my breath toward chance and/or discovery. I squeezed out a vivid piece of art but changed the perspective of the objects on display, shattering the vase, toppling the glass, animating the squirrel, breaking the candle, and scrambling those eggs.

Ta da, I reveled in my own artistry. I did what the assignment was and went even beyond. I took valuable steps toward my future endeavors. I surpassed even my own expectations and loved that I was inside those moments of creative mastery. I am not sure what the teacher made of me.

I was chasing that illusive muse of my life, one I still run after. At times we connect and stay in constant step. At other times she eludes me so I scrawl or sprawl or crawl toward artful output in any way I can.

While I understand that there are no rules to follow any more, there is only the need to reach toward the miracle of flowering bulbs, my amaryllis of continuing artistic and creative endeavors. All to transform my soul, my garden, and fill my heart.

Pens move across sacred white lines.

Pens slog toward truth and daring.

Thoughts pour through ink to sentences.

Silent wrestling. Chosen words. Careful Edit.

Feasting along with
Love, full heart and yearning
Toward the dessert.

Pray for direction
From anyone who may listen.
Seek advice to change.

A COURAGEOUS ACT
PREVIOUSLY PUBLISHED ON THE POETS AND WRITERS BLOG, MARCH 14, 2016

We writers gather close around the table, buoyed along by our continuing bravery. Not because we have each had our cancer battles but because we bravely face blank pages again and again. There is courage in our pens, our prose spilling onto our notebook paper. We face our pain, our past, and our present with scrawled imagination.

The time to be heroes is now, when the prompt has been given and the scratch of pens unites. We hum along, intent, working, concentrating, as the air duct hums along above us too. We are silent, reaching toward the perfect word or any word that describes or harnesses the beast. Oh rise up to us, dear muse, gather us toward a timed salvation. Give us this half hour of life, dripping and dropping or drowning upon the page.

Real or imagined, our lives are entwined within the hallowed pools of spilled ink, shards of dreams and delights wanting to be read aloud. Carry us along the timeless highway of connection. Do we all hover over our process or do we sail full-bodied toward a new happening, a new pronunciation, or a new verb. A new definition of closeness comes forth from our writing pose. We are humbled or overjoyed by the perfect word choice; one that comes in a flash yet has a very deep hidden meaning from some vivid past experience.

Cosmic rays of intelligence streak across the margins, coloring our lives with magic, hope, and truth. Do we dare to be so bold and blunt and to run wildly to the edge of sanity? Of course, we need the catharsis of earned sentences. We need the healing of combined stories. We just need to make shit up.

Come on bold prince of black ink; earn your way across a boundary of paper. Churn and turn out endless drafts of optimism or cheeky promise. Fill me up with longing for more communal escape. Do not let me down by running out of things to say. Our world waits in awe for this experiment in truth. The world within this writers group gropes forward to satisfy the wait, to acknowledge the awe, and to continue a dialog with the universe.

Time seems to stand still as penmanship erodes to blurs and barely formed missives. Yet time speeds up as breath is baited and imaginations fired by plucking from our dreams or sentimental wanderings. Be still our hearts as we transfer life forces to blue-lined commitment. Just continuing to dive into the narrative can right all.

The planets lend their full support, the gods look down upon the labor with admiration, and long-held truths are being laid bare. Simple connections between humans are being honored and trusted amid the pushing forward of language.

Exhaustion, emotion, exhalation, exquisite. All the senses are full and alive and driving toward one final statement.

My writing friends and heroes surround me now, excited by the closeness and the exertion, sliding toward a complete piece. Tranquility sets in as the closure sentence rounds out. We have beat back the day's blues by committing full disclosure and continuing our courage.

And for a brave finale we shall read aloud our work. It is amazing to behold and be part of such acts of heroism.

It Was No Accident; It Was an Accident

It was no accident that it was an accident. A particularly timed collision of personalities needing to express themselves at a time of great need in their lives. A gathering of souls collected to write.

The connecting medical threads are for some, dramatic, heightened, immediate, and all have a measured focused battle toward being whole. Each person turning pain shards into word gems, wisdom from each individual champion, which they impart on the collective group.

His story is uplifting
Her story is amazing.
We have all endured.
He'll rally, I hope.
While, she might come undone.

My experience is vastly different from the others, but the shared pen slash-and-bare-all determination connects us to this gathering of humanity.

We deliver the story of our health, a fiercely regarded commodity, in simple yet true prose. We possess our story. We delve into the giant maw of the illness industry by laying down our ink-stained description of anxiety. Sometimes we channel our anger. Can we trust our experiences will be measured against the passing of time?

Some of us will bury our memories with this pen and paper.

We'll slog through to the other side of medical jargon, jotting down impersonal confusing procedures. We'll make glib mention of jokes here and there. Altered states of dark humor offered up for shock value.

Dare we compare notes? I can't handle your distress. Our pens climb us to a rallying cry of: enough. We breathe along the margins. Being prompted to remember details means being delivered back to immediate and deep distractional fog.

Pen strokes to obliterate some fears.

Black and blue only from the ink flow now. Bruised flesh left behind as good health checkups flounce upon the steady march of time.

Deliver news. Reclamation of self, coming five pages in.

It is no accident that it was an accident that a writers group formed in a cancer ward.

Isaac Read

Fifty-six

In two days. I am fifty-six. Ten years back I was lost. I knew not. Lived in head. Heart was broken. Almost always angry. I knew not. Two years ago. Cancer found me. Start to change. Still a bit angry. Eight months ago. Heart broken again. One month ago. Miracle has happened.

Mind heart united. Heart mind united. Present to myself. Wherever I go. Mind heart together.

Peace is here. Courage is here. Strength is here. Joy is here. Hope is here. Mind heart together.

They share everything. Fifty six be wonderful.

SUE RIBNER

She was a gracious, very strong woman. Weeks before she died I called her because I had not heard from the writing class in a while. She told me that she was not teaching the class anymore, but she did not tell me how bad she was. I shared with her a quote about writing that I heard on a TV show. The quote is "Writing is an act of faith, not an act of grammar." I told her that it is so true because sometimes or all the time until I harness the skill I start writing something not knowing what I am going to say about the topic, and once I start writing out of that act of faith, ideas and images come to my mind and through pen to the paper.

Writing is an act of faith, and like in all acts of faith, there is fear that must be overcome through trust in your self as a writer.

Sue liked the quote and the comment I made about it. Weeks later when I came to the Writing, I was surprised to hear that she passed away. Tonight on the way to visit my brother as I was walking on Central Park West, I look up at the beautiful blue sky and I thought about Sue and said to myself, "She was a good soul" and I said a prayer for her.

RESILIENCE

I had a very difficult childhood, but still I have a child within, and despite what he went through, he has survived, and he is alive and well. He has a spirit that cannot be broken.

Who is the child?
The one that keep dreams alive.
The strong unconquerable spirit of freedom.
The one that believes in the future.
The one that trusts and loves.
He has hope and faith in God.
He connects with the imagination.
He can live in a mental space where there is no time.
He can live in playfulness.
He is very close to the heart.
He is in touch with his instincts.
He has a resolute survival spirit.
The child lives in the reality of the emotions.
He is vulnerable and strong.

Prudence

Mother, in my life in the past,
I talked too much with everybody.
You have covered me with the veil of your silence and I have overcome this.
Thank you so very much for listening to me.
Now teach me the virtue of Prudence.
Because of this virtue you are the teacher par excellence
In order that I could be witness of your presence.

Life Is a Race

I saw a picture of Jesse Owens at the race in the 1936 Olympics Games
in Germany.

What is going in my brain as I saw this picture?
The right, logical part of my brain is saying:

1. Life is a race.
2. There is a goal.
3. There are a lot of people watching you race.
4. You must have goal in life.
5. There is a lot of competition in this race.
6. The goal is to win the first place.

The left side of my brain is saying:

OK, I agree life is race, but it is also a dance.

YES! There is a goal, but my goal is to have peace, happiness, and smiles while I am pursuing the goal.

Agree, because life must be shared and emotions, feelings, imagination, and passions are what unites us.

Agree, but I am determined by the goal, not by someone else.

Agree, but it must be a friendly competition.

Yes, I Agree but it does not have to be first place. As a matter of fact, I do not care in what place I finish. My goal is to finish the race.

FREE HEART

You must soon have to go down to the deep.
Have faith that you will not go as one soul.
Others will go also with all the love you need.
People had gone broken in pieces and come whole.

When you go to that place you will surprise.
It is not as dark and scary as you thought.
You will see a lot of good and bad things.
That will allow you to finally realize they are not.
In the deep you will see the need to suffer.
So you can finally feel life as it should be.
Because suffering is a part of life that teaches you
To grow, to mature, to be strong, to be free.
So have courage and go down to the deep indeed,
Which is your heart that Jesus Christ had set free.

Joanne Rogovin

HEROES

WITH THE DEATH OF NELSON Mandela, I've been thinking about heroes.

The brilliant psychologist Donald Winnicott stated simply, "home is where we start from."

That is certainly true for me, raised in a home where caring for the underserved, left-wing politics, and general disdain for authority were the way we saw the world.

I don't have many heroes, and not surprising my first hero was my father, which is interesting because he wasn't very good at the job of being a dad. However, he was a brilliant, ethical, and just man, who fought hard for the things he believed in and taught me to do the same. He left prescription money with his patients who were struggling, he advocated for people who were being wrongly treated, and he was vocal in his praise of those who took unpopular stands.

I remember once, my Father went to court to appeal what he felt was an unfair parking ticket. The judge asked him if he wasn't making a fuss over a five-dollar ticket. My father's response was, "Judge are you here to mete out justice or am I keeping you from your golf game?" Case dismissed.

The model for life which he gave me were "Rules Are Meant to Be Broken," and "Respect Must Be Earned." He earned the respect of others by the example he set. He was a doctor who refused to join the AMA because he believed it was a fascist organization. He was a strong advocate for socialized medicine and never refused to care for those who could not pay.

Eleanor Roosevelt was adored in my home. A very shy young woman orphaned by the time she was ten, she had steel in her. She said, "No one can make you feel inferior without your consent." Wow. She said, "You must do the things you think you cannot do," and she did. She had a wonderful sense of humor: "A woman is like a teabag—you can't tell how strong she is until you put her in hot water." I wasn't even born when she made it possible for Marian Anderson to sing at the Lincoln Memorial, but I heard about them both. Her influence on FDR to create programs for the needy is immeasurable. The commitment she made to strengthen the UN in its early years, when it did seem like our best hope for peace, was dynamic and unwavering, and her insistence on creating the High Commission on

Human Rights has impacted untold numbers. More personally, she was my perfect model of what a woman could be—brave, smart, embracing, nonjudgmental. When the armed forces refused to let the Tuskegee Airmen fly in World War II, she went to their base to show her support, and I'll bet you know what happened next.

I had the great honor of interviewing her for my HS newspaper. We met at her gorgeous town house on East 65th Street in Manhattan. She was late and her Scotties kept me company. She had been at a football game at West Point and arrived with the largest yellow chrysanthemum I've ever seen pinned to her lapel. She was all apologies and offers of tea as I sat starstruck. I was truly in the presence of greatness, and, like so many of the people I admire, there was no arrogance, no posturing, just a deep commitment to making the world better.

My next addition to this small roster of champions is Pete Seeger. His ability to not waver from his convictions, to go to jail for his beliefs, and to stay the course is a wonder to me. I recently learned that there was a bill before Congress in 1943 to send all Japanese and Japanese Americans back to Japan after the war. Seeger, as an Army private, protested it, and the fact that he was engaged to a Japanese woman, the steadfast Toshi, brought him to the attention of the FBI. My family loathed and reviled Joe McCarthy and his henchmen: Martin Dies, Roy Cohn, and Richard Nixon. I had a close friend with equally left-wing parents, and we watched the HUAC hearings nearly every day after school. We hooted and hollered every time Pete showed his disdain for these ludicrous proceedings. And then there was that voice, clear and unwavering. He used music to tell our story and open our hearts, to dignify humanity and expose greed and deceit and corruption. Ticky-tacky boxes for houses, soldiers gone to graveyards, jounalists in the pockets of politicians. Nobody made it more real than Pete.

Wikipedia lists Nelson Mandela's occupation as "Activist, Politician, "Philanthropist, and Lawyer." How about world changer, revolutionary, humanist, exemplary leader. This man came out of twenty-seven years in prison with reconciliation in his heart, with an unwillingness to let his beloved country devolve into violent civil war. He learned and changed from his original reliance on violence to a commitment to dialogue and collaboration. He created the Truth and Reconciliation Commission to investigate human rights abuses during—and after—Apartheid. He was South Africa's "Washington and Lincoln rolled into one." I'll bet he heard Eleanor Roosevelt say, "the choices we make are ultimately our own responsibility." He was a rule breaker when the rules were unjust, a leader who earned the respect not just of his supporters but of his enemies.

His is the only ticker tape parade I've ever attended. His smile beaming, the crowd swooning with adoration for a real hero, not someone who hit a ball over a fence. He seemed almost bashful, a deep humility apparent to me. We need his like more than ever.

I miss him.

Eve Roshevsky

THE BRILLO CHRONICLES
I. ADVENTURES OF THE WONDER CAT

MOUSE IN MIDDLE OF THE carpet yesterday. Tail and hindquarters intact, head bloody, tho' attached. Rewarded Brillo for her offering with a Temptations treat.

Mice are rampant in this otherwise respectable and well-maintained building that we share with a high-end, doorman-equipped cooperative. With all the construction in this trendy neighborhood, the rodents must be on the move.

I'm not squeamish, after time spent in a rugged kibbutz in the hills of Jerusalem, reached by a frightening Egged bus ride from Israel's holiest city (you know: sanctity in every stone). Tsuba was merely a collection of wooden shacks with an avid—read, hungry— population of field mice. A family of them sought shelter nesting in the suitcase under my bed and would come out and play, racing around the room to entertain me during afternoon siesta. They liked the cookies and tomatoes I filched from the communal dining hall.

But back to Brillo: I'm pondering how I've managed to snuggle each night in bed beside a predator all these years!

II. Second Kill

A baby this time. Same spot on the carpet. No evidence of violence this time. Maybe it died of shock.

I know now how they get in! Last night I saw Brillo watching in the corner, under the sunset-and- Fairway-facing-window, her tail switching back and forth (always a bad sign)...And I knew what to expect when, getting out of bed, I stepped on something squishy on the carpet. And there s/he/it was, tail protruding. I plastic-bagged it, resisting the temptation to show it off at breakfast and consigned it to a garbagy grave.

III. Trouble

We've had a very tough time recently, Brillo *et moi*.

One day she began throwing up everything. Her tiny gray, furry body convulsed with waves of muscle contractions. A delicate, though pathetic retching sound alerting me late at night that I'd find another brown stain on the carpet in the morning.

Rabbi Ari, the cat whisperer, says he loves her, she's so sweet... yet he hasn't seen her fierce side. When annoyed, biting my arm time and again when I fall asleep reading while stroking her. Stalking prey, leaving bloodied or headless mice as presents for me on the carpet as I wake in the morning.

And now, possibly string-like mouse intestine under the TV table—I haven't looked too closely at it and will ask cat-fancier Sergio, our over-educated porter (who did his master's at Union Theological Seminary), to come for it.

IV. Recovery

Brillo in the corner: Stalking mice? Hiding from medication? Or just being unfriendly?

Brillo on the bed: Curled up sleeping so peacefully atop Machu Picchu on the Peruvian blanket, the shades of gray and brown complementing her Russian not-really-Blue fur.

*Thank you, Raul, for that wonderful blanket
that's travelled with me all these years.*

And thank you, Brillo, for all the time we have had together—you are my best friend, my roommate, my soul mate, my muse. I don't want to live without you, and don't want you to suffer, yet where do we draw the line?

You'll tell me and I will listen, with love and respect, as always...

V. Xmas Edition

Visited Brillo at the veterinary hospital today. First she hissed at me, later sat in my lap.

It was a joy to see her 'tho she was pissed—so would I be with a catheter in my leg.

Hopefully home tomorrow, then subcutaneous hydration, antibiotics, and appetite stimulant. We'll do it with the help of valium, perhaps, and maybe she'll warm my bed again tomorrow night: the best Xmas present ever!

VI. Brillo's Last Day

At breakfast, as per usual: Louise moaning and groaning. Robin's fruity voice mimics Garbo's acting. Pam is absent and didn't return my calls yesterday. Won't call now as she sleeps through breakfast.

I can't expect support from anyone here because everyone's unhappy, all wrapped up in their particular tsuris, misery, pain. So, it was just the two of us.

Back in our room, Brillo threw up her favorite food. Joanie helped me load her into her elegant pink carrier to take her to the vet for a final visit.

After consulting with Rabbi Ari and Marilyn the vet tech and Marilyn's boss, all agreed: A kidney infection needing continued antibiotics. We would have to raise the money for it (and torture her further to administer it).

I couldn't do that and told them to go ahead…

Waited for the injection…

Then the doctor pumped her full of the poison …

And she went to sleep in my lap.

VII. After Brillo

Slept alone last night for first time in years without Brillo.

My roommate for eight of them, my muse for three.

My comfort and refuge from this dreary place.

Lara Stein

I LEARNED ABOUT EMILY'S WRITING workshop during a checkup at the cancer center a year and a half after finishing treatment. My experience still felt so raw that I was reluctant to step foot in the same medical facility if I didn't have a doctor's appointment. But the lure of a writing workshop proved more powerful, and I went, glad to have the opportunity to process my experience through a kinder, gentler Write Treatment. This short piece was written in response to a photographic prompt, "The Ballet of the Photographers at a Windswept Mountain Top in Hawaii," taken in 1954 by Lucien Aigner, which captured my feelings as a patient.

UNDER THE LENS

Their cameras are poised, their bodies tensed in pursuit of their subject, their photograph. They own this moment. They stand with legs apart, firmly braced, a sturdy stance. Backs arch behind them, anything for the best angle, counterbalanced by those legs, steady, unyielding, heading off any tumbling or tipping. They are not the vulnerable ones. They come in from all angles, examining their subject, poking, prodding, questioning, capturing. One photographer has already stopped, feverishly reloading his film for more. One man has turned away and pointed his lens toward the opposite horizon, searching for new layers of meaning, new subjects. And what of the subject herself? Where is she? Her body here, perhaps, under the lens, but her pure presence hovering, taking flight, untethered by the demands of the cameraman. A mere lens cannot capture her spirit, cannot know the inner workings of her mind. Above, the clouds pass by, expansive, free, all knowing.

ALL IN A DAY'S WORK

"Horrible, isn't it?" says the genetic counselor, striding down a labyrinthine hallway, her back to me. "Horrible" comes out as "harrable," strangled by a New York accent and attitude, the indignities of urban life piling up like a personal affront. Something is always "harrable" in the city. She ushers me into her office and shuts the door.

She is referring to the weather, apparently—the rising mercury, the summer heat index—that is horrible, not the personal inferno; I've been sweating the past two days. I am thirty-six, and I have a three-year-old child. I can measure the time since my cancer diagnosis in hours—less than forty-eight.

My newly shell-shocked world is the elephant in the room, never referenced during our two-hour counseling session. We are in a suite seven floors up from the sweltering pavement; the office is perfectly climate controlled.

Clean Tupperware litters her desk, the detritus of a routine day, forkfuls of salad for lunch followed by spoon-feeding statistics all afternoon—flipping charts, comparing prognoses of patients with BRCA1 and BRCA2 mutations, floating clinical terms like "chemotherapy" and "prophylactic hysterectomy." Each situation is hypothetical; my coin toss is still up in the air.

I'm searching for a thread I can weave from the life I once knew to this strange new world, when I remember having genetic testing while pregnant with my son. It turned up no Tay Sachs, no mysteriously named maple syrup urine disease. The memory is oddly comforting, until the counselor, a new mother herself, leans forward and whispers in a conspiratorial voice, "You know, BRCA mutations have no bearing on childhood cancers."

In her single unscripted moment, she unwittingly twists the knife, introducing a horror far greater than a hypothetical hysterectomy. Her attempt at mother-to-mother understanding is genuine, a real stab at human connection that our counseling session lacked. She reaches out as a mother, an experience we share in common, but she can't connect as a cancer patient. We are on opposite sides of the same horrible desk.

GALLOPING THROUGH DARKNESS

We got rained out, yet we got lucky.

Fat raindrops fell on the Jersey shore that summer Saturday, but we hit the boardwalk arcade and won a prize, tokens spilling from the twenty-five-cent slot machine. I hit the jackpot again that night, finding a lump in my breast, a bump that trilled beneath my fingertips. When my body sounded an alarm, I stopped to listen, and for this I am grateful.

I had breast cancer at age thirty-six, and still, I was lucky. I pulled through, and my husband and young son got lucky, too. As the refrain in the classic Dr. Suess story goes: "Did I ever tell you how lucky you are?"

As a family, we held on to that plastic prize horse for dear life, the inch-tall trinket from the arcade that marked a major turning point in our lives. Together we galloped through darkness and kept on going, where it was lighter and brighter. The diagnosis gave way to surgeries and chemo. Baldness gave way to hair. Constant worries gave way to not thinking about the C-word for days.

Along the way, well-meaning friends and acquaintances told me they were sorry, or they were angry, even though their feelings did not always mirror mine. What could I say? "Thanks for feeling sorry for me?" Or "Thanks for your anger?" No, thanks.

Instead, I replied brightly, "Oh, it's OK. I was lucky, I caught it early." Then I would keep rattling off my script: "I'll get through treatment and if the cancer never comes back, I'll be fine."

"If." That tiny, two-letter conditional word snuck itself inside my breezy little speech. "If."

I was lucky now, yes, but what...if...? What then? I didn't care to think about it.

Instead, I tried to ignore the "if" and live my life—the life that I was here to live, and grateful to have. To wear, without a lick of irony, my "Luckiest Shirt Ever!," ordered from Threadless because it had a rabbit's foot, wishbone, horseshoe, ladybug, four-leaf clover, Maneki-Neko, number seven, and a shooting star printed across the chest. I even wore the snug-fitting tee in those early postsurgery days, when my boobs were uneven, off-kilter from one another. No shrinking behind a baggy sweatshirt for me. I put on that tee shirt and walked my son to school, took him to the park, and read him bedtime stories at night. And that Dr. Seuss book came back to haunt me.

"You ought to be thankful, a whole heaping lot, for the places and people you're lucky you're not!"

The book's lovable Duckie is a sweet boy with a delightful tuft of orange hair, but that's not enough to make him lucky. It's only by comparison, to those "muchly much-much more unlucky than you," that Duckie's star shines so brightly.

He's not, for instance, Herbie Hart, who, with his terribly complex, taken-apart Throm-dim-bu-lator, makes for great rhymes of woe in the talltale world. But in the real world, I know people, for real, who will never "know if the Gick or the Goor fits into the Skrux or the Snux or the Snoor."

"Sisters" who don't know which toxic cocktail will kick their breast cancer cells to the curb. Shall we try Adriamycin/Cytoxan/Taxol or perhaps Methotrexate? By gack, we can't quite tell, and no, we'll never know for sure whether the Skrux or the Snux was the fix you desperately needed.

Our lucky Duckie is also not, thank heavens, Farmer Falkenberg's seventeenth radish, whose ominous fate is foreshadowed by a wide-eyed worm slithering past radishes number one through sixteen. That sinking feeling is one my breast cancer sisters—"one in eight" statistics come to life—know all too well.

And God forbid that Duckie is "a left sock, left behind by mistake in the Kaverns of Krock!" Who knows what else you might find tucked away in a neighboring cavern; perhaps a woman's left breast, cut off by a surgeon, but not by mistake, and discarded into the nether regions of who knows where? There it is, a loose boob next to a lost tube sock in the Kaverns of Krock.

That my good luck, or anyone's luck, hangs on the (mis)fortune of another makes me squirm. I feel as woozy as if I'd run smack into Herbie Hart's Throm-dim-bu-lator. Or as if I'd chanced upon a crumple-horn, web-footed, green-bearded Schlotz, its tail knotted in inextricable knots by our favorite wordsmith Dr. Seuss.

But to pause for a moment, silencing the Throm-dim-bu-lator and taking a deep breath.... To stay on the page, and look that green-bearded Schlotz in the eye, is to dispel the discomfort of the "if" and start conquering the fear of the unknown. To acknowledge that recurring fear of the Schlotz ambling close enough to swish its tail against your legs is to acknowledge the fear of another brush with illness.

Unwinding those wily knots of fear is to start dissolving any "lucky/unlucky" dichotomy. Getting to know the crumple-horn creature herself means making no comparisons, and simply having compassion for another's journey—your journey and my journey and her journey. Honoring someone's path means radiating love and supporting her way, rather than shrinking away. It means locking eyes with a survivor, and listening with care, without flinching or casting eyes downward, when she shares what her bumps in the road are like.

To pause for a moment, silencing the Throm-dim-bu-lator, is to be present. To be present is to honor life and the randomness of it all, while sending love across the spectrum of our sisters, no matter our circumstances. Whether we are Herbie Hart, Farmer Falkenberg's radish, or that lucky Duckie, all we have—all that any of us ever have—is this moment. Right now, right here, we are together and we are alive. In this moment, we are all lucky to be here.

GO ASK ALICE

She survived Wonderland—and you can survive Cancerland

There it is—cancer—the news you can't wrap your head around. The shock, the sudden decisions, the leaps of faith. But you emerge, finally, holding the key that unlocks your treatment plan. You walk through that door, to the OR, the infusion suite, or who knows where, amazed you didn't hit your head on the way in.

Alice "*came upon a low curtain she had not noticed before, and behind it was a little door about fifteen inches high: she tried the little golden key in the lock, and to her great delight it fitted!*"

You duck through this most unexpected door and keep going. When the going gets tough, you get tougher. You stomach side-effects of treatment and navigate unexpected roadblocks. You stumble, but you pick yourself back up. It's free fall down the rabbit hole, but you land on your own two feet.

"'*Well!' thought Alice to herself, 'after such a fall as this, I shall think nothing of tumbling down stairs! How brave they'll all think me at home!'*"

They call you a survivor now, and there's a good reason for that. You're brave, to be sure, but life itself is a brave new world, and it's scary to imagine what's next.

Alice "*waited for a few minutes to see if she was going to shrink any further: she felt a little nervous about this; 'for it might end, you know,' said Alice to herself, 'in my going out altogether, like a candle.'*"

Will cancer, or the treatment itself, snuff out your flame? Dark thoughts cross your mind and then vanish. You fell down the rabbit hole, but you're not currently six feet under, so you keep living your life. You keep chasing the White Rabbit, one pocket-watch ticktock at a time.

Chasing these adventures in Wonderland, you feel a twinge and phone your doctor. Perhaps you hear reassuring words right then or wait for test results. It comes to pass that a bruise is a bruise, and a sore leg simply a sports injury. It's not cancer that has returned, but life that has circled round, simply and gloriously, to its mundane existence once again.

Alice "was quite surprised to find that she remained the same size: to be sure, this generally happens when one eats cake, but Alice had got so much into the way of expecting nothing but out-of-the-way things to happen"

Without "drink me" and "eat me" potions, life is strangely ordinary; some might even say a little plain. Perhaps not entirely back to normal, but good and quiet again.

And yet. If there was a magic "do-over" button on the story of your life, would you cut cancer from the picture? Probably, but maybe not. It's given you unbelievable adventures: croquet with the Queen, Cheshire cat's famous grin, and psychedelic mushrooms from a Caterpillar. It's given you new perspective and some silver linings you never expected.

As Alice reflected: "I almost wish I hadn't gone down that rabbit-hole—and yet—and yet—it's rather curious, you know, this sort of life!"

You have taken this curious life, and you are living it. This life that is infinitely more interesting, and all the more precious, for surviving your own adventures in wonderland.

Caroline Marie Sun
July 20, 1962–December 9, 2014

CAROLINE CAME TO THE WRITE *Treatment Workshops beginning in 2012 and was a regular participant until her health made it difficult to attend. She was a committed, colorful, and precise writer with a deep well of empathy, intelligence, and artistic instinct. She is sorely missed. Thank you to her husband, Anthony DeLuca, for the support to include her work. She is pictured here holding her beloved kitty, Po.—ER*

THE ENCOUNTER

I didn't really notice her for quite some time. The view from the outdoor balcony of the Sands Point estate dominated my perception, and I was too busy watching the wave crests of the Long Island Sound hitting the rocky shore. It was quite breezy, even the shiny black cormorants were staying on the wooden remains of the old pier—not venturing to dive, get all wet, and then climb out to dry in the chilly air.

The sun was already slanting in that late-September way so the shadow of the house (or really I should say the "mansion") was already creeping halfway across the lawn. The sunlight hit the farthest half with warmth, but that made the shadowy near end even more frigid.

As we walked back toward the house, I passed a large balustrade, about waist high, of some kind of grayish stone or cement. Early leaves had already begun to fall, although most of the trees were still quite well attired. So it was not surprising to see some fluttering movement out of the corner of my eye every few moments as a breeze came through.

But one momentary quiver caught my eye, different from the rest. Pale, green-gray, like a dried spring leaf, the preying mantis sat poised, quietly, on the stone. A flicker now and then of her wing epaulets, but otherwise not a move. Her delicate celadon limbs caught in an Eastern fight pose.

At first I thought she's dead, poor thing—end of summer, winter on the way, probably froze in place just as the cold winds had begun to sail in from the north. I decided that I wanted to take her picture. I scrunched down to her level to get a better image in the viewfinder. I snapped a shot: it didn't come out too well, a bit fuzzy perhaps because of the shakiness of my hand or perhaps because of the rustling of her wings?

So I tried again. This time something *did* move—it was her eyes. Her tiny, black-dot eyes moved around in their big green orbs. She was looking right at me!

I stepped back a bit startled, and sure enough, her gaze followed me. I walked slowly to the left and then slowly to the right, and still her eyes tracked my movements. But now she began to twist her head and even moved a little as I moved out of range of her little black pupils.

I was both excited and astonished: one, because I had never been this close to a mantis before; two, because she was right out in the open with no protective greenery, no discreet organic flotsam and jetsam to hide any part of her; and three, she was still alive and interacting directly with me.

I began to take several shots of her from all angles. I tried to shoot quickly because I feared that at any moment she would flex her wings and fly away. She did shift her leg position once or twice, but otherwise, she was a perfect model. All the while, there were other visitors on the lawn, but none paid any attention to me, what I was doing, or whom I was doing it with.

It was just a private moment between the mantis and me. She stayed put, and we eventually left as the shadows began to deepen and darken. I thought to myself: was she a *preying* mantis waiting and watching for her next meal or a *praying* mantis communing with an alien being as the season of her life came to a close. Either way, she was a small, fragile miracle to me on a brisk and cold September day.

Lightning Bolts

Lightning strikes once—a strange occurrence: shocking, surprising, out of the blue. We talk about it like it is rare and unique, but it happens all the time, all around the planet, thousands of times a day. And yet to see a bolt do it right in front of you, when you cannot predict it, cannot really imagine it, and then it just happens.

The closer it is, the more powerful and instantaneous the rumble that reverberates over you, through you, shaking the foundations of your chest and stomach. Blinding you with sight and deafening sound. But then it is gone. It moves on from where you are standing, or sitting, or staring, or looking. Another flash and rumble, further away, moving in another space and time, receding from you. Slowly it heads into the distance and then is seen and heard no more. But lightning can and does strike twice and sometimes more than even that.

Now it is a different story. It is aiming at you; it will not let you go this time. It is waiting in the darkness undercover, waiting for the moment to strike again. This time it is aiming at your vitals. You cannot see or hear it coming, but you feel it. You know something is not right, something is about to knock you down again. You hope, against hope, that this storm will pass over quickly, leaving nothing but distant echoes and shimmers of light behind. But we humans have harnessed the power of those bolts in CAT scans, MRIs, and PET scans. Now we train those powers on our fragile, moist, vulnerable selves, turn the beams on, and see what sparks fly. Another turn of the circle in the "doughnut-shaped" machines seals my fate. Lightning has struck me again—both where it hit before and also in a new location, shattering my lower spine with fracture, fatigue, and searing pain. Now I need the painkillers and steroids for real: to be able to sit, to bend and tie my shoe, to roll into and out of the bed, to try to wash my feet in the shower.

Lightning knows no mercy. She strikes with precision and ruthlessness. Her skill is almost surgical, and yet catastrophic in her damage. I am numb with this new onslaught—hating the universe for hitting me down again when I was just starting to feel that things were looking up, alternating with a sense of doom and a sense that there is nothing I can do as I am once again carried along, helplessly, on a sea of chemotherapy, radiation, and surgery.

Where is my agency in all this? Where are **my thunderbolts**? Oh that I had a quiver full of them like the Greek god Zeus that I could grab and hurl at the demons that now beset me. I need Hephaestus to smith them out for me with his band of mighty Cyclops—electric blue-and-pink bolts to counteract and heal the damage that these new blasts have done to me. Oh Prometheus, bring them gently to me with a bow of gold that I might take sure and steady aim.

What If...

What if I could actually talk to my cat Enoki? What would he talk about? Would he complain about the food we give him and tell us what flavors he prefers? Would he tell us precisely how and when he likes to be petted and cuddled, or when he can't take all the noise we make with the vacuum cleaner, the music we play, or the television we watch.

He might tell us about his feelings with his new kitten companions, Phineas and Coco—how he likes their company, but sometimes they are a little too rambunctious and young for him as they tear about the apartment knocking things over. Or he might tell us about his former companions: his beloved Luna, whose shiny black fur contrasted so sharply against his own gray and white. How they enjoyed lying next to one another, arms intertwined, or putting their necks and heads together like lovers. Sometimes they would lay nose to tail, making a ying-yang sign of black, white, and gray fur in a round fuzzy ball.

I know he would talk about how much he loved Po and Mookie, the two orange-and-white spotted tabbies whom we found together as brothers. Enoki might tell us how much he enjoyed raising them and treating them as his own kittens. How they followed his every move and included him in their playful adventures and looked up to him as a "god." But then Enoki might reveal the details of the terrible night of the fire that took the lives of Luna and Po. He would describe what he saw and heard, and what he did that preserved his life when we thought all was lost. He was terrified at the noise and confusion of the firefighters breaking all the windows, ripping holes in the walls, overturning furniture and doors. How did Enoki endure and survive that? And when it was all over, how he crept up to the attic to hide. Yet he must have trusted we were still around because he came down and saw and ate the bowl of fresh food and water I left in his usual spot in the shambles of the kitchen. His relief at being able to eat and drink, and his hope that we would be back to find him.

What were his thoughts when he saw Tony working his way through the debris of the attic, calling "Enoki." Enoki, too traumatized to respond, stayed put, and even when Tony found him and could see his face, Enoki crept even farther away. Was he angry at us for not being there when the fire happened? Was he afraid he was "imagining" Tony, but it was not real. Finally, when Tony grabbed his smoke-stained body and screamed downstairs to me, "Enoki was alive"—what was going through Enoki's mind then: relief, joy, fear, anger, sadness?

What if Enoki could speak to us—perhaps he would not say any of the things I just outlined. Maybe he would want to talk about philosophy and the cosmos. Or ask about the world outside the window. Or get into discussions with us about the music we play or the shows we watch. Or ask about the meaning of life and why humans behave as they do.

He is such a sensitive soul that I am sure he would surprise us with what he knows and understands. I just want him to know how much we love him and how we marvel every day at the "miracle" of his still being here with us.

NAMING THE KITTY

She was a classic tan tabby with dark black and tan swirls all over her head, limbs, and body. They were so richly marbles that I used to call her my little "fudge swirl ice cream" girl. In addition, she had short silky black fur on her legs, and when she stretched them way out, both to flex them and to give them a good licking, we called them her "black stockings." She was tiny when we got her at the North Shore Animal League. So tiny that she could sit in the palm of one hand without other support. But she soon won our hearts by climbing with her tiny little claws up our sweaters to perch on our shoulders. Of course, there was a teeny tiny "mew" that went with those sharp, bright-green eyes.

As they took her from the room so that we could adopt her, the volunteers, a group of fresh-faced teenage hoping-to-be veterinarians one day, started passing around the message: "They are taking Samantha. Samantha has a new home!" Samantha had a special tag on her collar because it turned out that she had had a sore on her tongue and needed daily medication—which is why the volunteers were so happy that we were willing to take the small bundle of fur. We were still pretty new to having cats—we had also adopted a kitten the year before—so getting the medication into such a tiny being twice a day was quite a challenge. We decided that "Samantha" did not really suit her, so we tried out a number of different names over the course of the next week: tiger, missy, cupcake, when finally my husband asked me about my childhood nicknames. One of them was "Anee," which meant "child number two," as I was the second daughter in a Chinese family. This name also fit our kitten because she was joining our household as our second cat.

The North Shore Animal League is very responsible about making sure their adopted animals are vaccinated and neutered at the appropriate time. We actually had to sign a contact and a definite date when we would bring Anee back for her surgery. Since "Anee" is a Chinese word, there is no definite accepted way to spell it, but I thought "A-N-E-E" worked. However, my husband was the one dropping the kitten off at the OR and picking her up later that evening, so he filled out the hospital forms.

Later that night, my husband came home very sheepish about picking up the kitten. Apparently, they called the owners up to collect their animals using the *pet's name* rather than the owner's first or last name. So Tony had sat in the waiting room with a group of other pet owners listening as names like "Muffin," "Fluffy," "Lucas," "Oreo," and others were called out by the young vet tech. But at one point, the vet tech came out nervously and called out "Anus"? Everyone in the room looked around in some surprise and consternation: "anus"? Who would call their pet "anus."

The young technician tried again a bit louder: "Anus"?

It suddenly dawned on my horrified husband that we had not agreed on the spelling of the kitten's name. He chose to write it down in the *French style* as "A-N-A-I-S." When he realized the young woman was talking about our kitty, he raised his hand shakily and red-faced and said loudly, "It is ANEE!"

Anee lived happily with us to the ripe-old cat age of nineteen.

THE MUSIC OF THE WORLD

Eight cycles per second—that is the "hum" of the electromagnetic background song of the Earth. A song punctuated by the thunderous crashes of lightning, life-threatening solar flares and winds from outer space, and everything from our great machines to the thin bands of our radio waves. We are all traveling within this hum, unconscious that it is all around us, encircling us, ringing throughout the planet and its atmosphere: a kind of "music" of the Earth chiming softly to its own celestial movement.

We, ourselves, are but electromagnetic beings with a given mass, shape, velocity, and direction (at least some of the time). Our very blood contains iron ore, the stuff of magnets, and the material that also is attracted to them. How can we not be affected by the north and south meridians connecting the Earth's great poles. And yet we move about in this "soup" of charged particles and aligned forces in total blindness and unaware.

But our fellow creatures are not as blind as we. Migrating birds feel these invisible pulses of radiation and use them to navigate across continents and oceans, both day and night. They have a special tiny organ in their brain that tells them where the magnetic meridians are. Insects have also been shown to alter their flight patterns in relation to a magnet close by. It is suspected that other mammals may possess this capability too. The compass itself shows that the power is there, even to move a small sliver of metal to point northward.

Perhaps some of us can see these forces too. There are people who claim to see "auras" around the human body—perhaps they have some special sensitivity in their brains that can pick up the electromagnetic fields that we generate and interact with, as they fluctuate with our strength and feelings throughout the night and day. We do track our heartbeats with EKGs (electrocardiograms), which we then depict as undulating waves on an oscilloscope. Metal nodes on our skin are used to pick up these faint electrical rhythms. Likewise, we even "jolt" a stopped heart to awaken by using controlled electrodes.

Yet why do we (as supposedly higher organisms) lack the facility of the birds (with their tiny brains) to detect this worldwide song?

Even to physicists, the very concept of electromagnetism has always been a mysterious force because the two are so deeply intertwined and inseparable from each other. Every wire with current passing through it also generates a small magnetic "field" around it. Conversely, the physical spinning of magnets, one in relation to another, is used to generate electricity. They are an indivisible pair: created only in the presence of both together.

So perhaps it is profoundly appropriate that the Earth's own hum is eight cycles a second, because the number eight is, itself, an intertwined figure like the electromagnetic force. And when the number eight is placed on its side it represents infinity—as in the nearly infinite hum of the planet.

Belinda Ward

SITUATION VACANT—GUARDIAN ANGEL: PREVIOUS EXPERIENCE NOT REQUIRED

I BELIEVE WE ALL HAVE guardian angels. How do I know? My friend Regine, a very spiritual, tarot-card reader extraordinaire told me so. It was late one afternoon, schlepping to the subway in the rain, from a battle-worn workday, when out of no-where she declared,

"Everyone has a guardian angel"

I agreed halfheartedly, too tired to discuss something I'd never considered, too busy dodging traffic and umbrellas. Even if I did believe, the way today had gone, and if I was keeping score, Disasters were leading eight guardian angels 0.

I hurried home, rain dripping down the back of my neck.

That evening, my new boyfriend got into the elevator and handed me a tiny scrap of screwed-up paper very matter-of-factly. Screwed up just about summed up the day was my first thought.

Inside this black-and-white crackled wrapping was a tiny metal guardian angel. At first I wondered why he choose this and what's wrong with flowers? I thanked him in the manner with which the gift was given. Simply. I stuffed it in my pocket along with three tissues and a sticky sweet stuck to a five-dollar bill, more interested in getting to a large gin and tonic.

The next day fumbling about looking for coffee money, I remembered the guardian angel conversation as I found the little metal angel. I'm sure it winked at me. It was a sign. A sign I tell you!

Sitting with coffee and playing my sister's favourite game "watching" (people), I pondered how many of these passersby believed or cared about the idea of a guardian angel. If they come out of nowhere that I now believe they do, then I'm sure they could be all shapes, sizes, and types. Maybe you could simply create and conjure up your own depending on the guardian job to be done.

Not to be greedy on the guardian angel front, I think I would like a guardian dragon today. Big tail, speaks five languages, must love full English breakfast (even full Irish will do), and get along with dogs. I don't care about hot, or for that matter, bad breath.

My mum says I have a vivid imagination, so conjuring up a dragon to crusade with is easy. I want a slayer of worry, of doubt, an attacker of mindless activity that provides little reward. A dragon to fight small fears that somehow become big at the most inconvenient moment. I would put my guardian dragon to work on the silly stupid little fears that lurk like silent dark monsters hiding around corners, skulking about, paralyzing untethered action. Swapping joy and abandonment for…"what ifs."

I'll find my dragon a place to live under the bed. Behind a pile of magazines, with a nice knitted blanket (dragons like to sleep on wool). I'll feed him sausages, crisps, and the occasional pie made by me dad and polish his scales with beeswax. I'll use his breath to keep my toes warm, his fire to fight at a moment's notice.

I'll call him Frederic the Fear Slayer.

"Dragon, smelly dragon breath"

"Sir Dragon burning bright"

Can you hear me?

Lost and Found

Another city on the speaking circuit. My husband, the professor—adored, smart, predicable, always on the road. I rarely have any desire to go with him. Actually…he's stopped asking.

He casually mentioned Rome over pot roast and mashed potatoes, and my mouth took over my hesitant brain.

"Take me with you."

He continued forking pot roast into the mouth that carefully considers everything.

"You'll be by yourself most of the time."

"That's fine I can find my way around."

"You'll be in a strange city."

"That's OK I was in Oxford last week and managed to find my way back."

After two days of chasing or gentle persuasion with roast beef dinners and red wine, I was booked.

Once there I left the worn splendor of the green and gold hotel, crawling out from under the remnants of room service. Rodney had already gone to his speaking engagement. I had my lire, my handbag, and my scarf tied in the style of Audrey Hepburn in Roman Holiday, feeling like the girl I'd left behind when I got married.

The streets buzzed, espresso machines steamed, scooters paupled as I experienced the ritual of standing up for morning coffee. I had read an article on what to buy in Rome. I wanted something that no one else in the book club would have, something unexpected—leather was top of the list. I stumbled into a side street, down a small alley, with aromas of lunch underway where I came to a window that was piled high with crisp white-printed paper bags. As my nose engaged with the glass, I realized that inside each bag was a pair of leather gloves. I walked in; this shop had obviously been looking after ladies for a very long time, I had no Italian. The contessa of the glove...no Inglese.

She appraised me, slowly took my arm, and rested my elbow on her worn marble counter, my hand pointing to the sky. She peered at me over her glasses, peered back at her kingdom of gloves, and came back with a pair of red gloves. Red...she looked at me and thought red. I was over the moon blushing like a bride. I couldn't pay quickly enough. She wrapped them carefully in brown paper, tied them with gold ribbon, and slid the package across the table with the ceremony of communion.

Where would I take my red leather gloves? I felt dizzy with excitement a pair of gloves had brought me back to me. I spotted a café alongside the Pantheon, a bit early for lunch, but I'm on holiday. A waiter in a jacket that matched the tablecloth fussed with an ashtray, my cue to order. I ordered the second cappuccino of the day and played watching as my sister calls it—people watching. I couldn't resist putting the gloves on for just a minute, to become an Italian signoria, just for a minute.

"May I sit down?"

I stared back. It's a man, an Italian man, coming to sit with me. Fuelled by glove fever I replied, "Yes, yes."

"I couldn't help but notice your gloves. They are beautiful."

I felt as though I knew him, he smelled familiar of cologne and coffee spice, his eyes teased. He ordered us both a negroni.

The next day, pinned on the café door…was a note flapping in the breeze and it said…

Found: One red leather glove, gold wedding ring inside.

Eloïse Watt

KRYPTONITE OF PLACE

"WHICH PLACE DO YOU LIKE best?" My husband and I are New Yorkers who now spend three quarters of our year in Scotland. Not the Scotland of castles and golf and single-malt, but a hardscrabble crofting community of seventy-some people in six thousand five hundred acres on the northernmost coast. I trot these statistics out every time I'm asked, as if they could answer the question. I mean at least apples and oranges are both fruit.

Sometimes when I can't sleep in the land of sheep, I find myself counting the bi-peds on the fivish-acre block we return to in Greenwich Village. I go building by building in my head, estimating the number of inhabitants, adding each number to the next. No matter how quickly I drift off, the total far exceeds seventy. So. On our block. In New York. Mega the population of our hangout in The Highlands. In one twelve-hundredth of the space. More statistics, but no idle exercise. If I can calculate the differences between the two lives I live, perhaps I can join them back together in some pacifying whole.

I arrived in New York in 1976, aged twenty-two, to be an actor. I presumed a number of things about my future: a thriving theatrical career within a few years, love with a fellow thespian perhaps a few years my senior, and to have a child before I turned thirty. I imagined having a boy and a girl eventually, though I was flexible and didn't insist on their order of arrival. I also imagined a lot of dues-paying and living in hovels, but eventually, I thought, the "we" in all this might be able to afford some getaway out of the city. I pictured a place in Connecticut or up in the Catskills. Tiny, you understand. I didn't consider any of this dreaming. I thought these expectations so modest; it never occurred to me they wouldn't fall neatly into line.

Well as it turned out, the thespian lover arrived on cue but we split up just after my thirtieth birthday. The acting career morphed into a decade and a half of teaching Shakespeare to other actors. And the escape from New York City didn't occur till many years later when I was forty-one and then involved a man with five grown children.

The haze of our courtship was technicolored by a trip to Scotland, where we each had ancestry. In the way of American branches of an ancient tree, we grew besotted with the place, married there, and returned from each trip wishing we'd spent more time. When my husband retired and I quit teaching, we bought a small house on the sparse rim of Scotland, closer to the Arctic Circle than London. The town was as plain a place as Manhattan was fancy. It was not a renunciation of New York but a compelling ache to expand toward something other.

It is only now, seven years on, that I've begun to assess how different this "other" is from what I started out wanting. My early dreams of a place away were founded on the centrifugal pull of a successful New York life. It would be both a continuum and a retreat, honed against the anchor of the city. And in fact my husband and I gave upstate a shot for a while, splitting our week between Manhattan and a millhouse two hours north. Before long we found ourselves with two full-time lives, each stuffed into half the time. It wore us out. And so our dream of somewhere else evolved into a place we would stay put for a regular stretch. We started out living six months a year in Scotland and six months in New York but déjà vu quickly convinced us that one place needed to be primary. New York was known. We settled on enough of a sliver of year in the city to visit family and friends, and almost nine months in our chosen idyllic setting. What I did not foresee was the way the choice would reshape my sense of the city I'd long staked my heart and soul on.

"New York's a nice place to live but you wouldn't want to visit there," I used to say, believing the city's true gifts only reveal themselves with full commitment. Now I am a visitor. I find myself increasingly out of the loop in a mecca where the loop is all important. Worse: I've lost much of my lust for the loop. Our life in Scotland is slowly shifting my—you should forgive the expression—values in uncomfortable, unurban directions. *THIS WASN'T PART OF THE DEAL*, a voice in me screams. *I'm a New Yorker! Hard-won, hardnosed: one of the self-choosing chosen...I never meant to secede!* How foolish to have expected my relationship to the molten center of the universe to remain fixed while I went off gallivanting.

Which place do I like best? I have grown cantankerous around the question. I'm with Whitman: *I am large. I contain multitudes...* Why can't I be big enough for both? So rank, this ache for ranking. Yet there is an issue here. The two places require such different parts of me—one receding, one developing. While it feels a betrayal to abandon one in favor of the other when we swap places, being both in both turns out to be surprisingly challenging.

When I was growing up, I loved the episode in which Superman was needed in two places at once. He used his strength to split his molecular being into twins, each distressingly mortal. Divided in half, he lost the essential powers of a unified self. So it feels to me. Who knew that the make-it-there-make-it-anywhere mastery of thirty years in Manhattan could prove so vulnerable?

I Was Alone on Christmas Day

I had spent a goodly chunk of the week before in Newtown, inside the mourning bubble of dear friends whose six-year-old boy had been slaughtered by a twenty-year-old boy with a semiautomatic weapon. There were places for me to be, but I didn't want to be with anyone. I needed time to digest and didn't feel I could do it eating and drinking in the company of others, however dear. I thought a lot about that bubble, about its strange insulating comforts, ironic under the circumstances: at the church, the food as far as the eye could see laid out by volunteers; the mutual friends of my friends, many of whom I had not seen in ages; the embraces, endless in number and length; and the only distant awareness of the lines outside, those standing in the cold for hours waiting to file in because they had to be there.

The television, when I turned it on, kept talking about the Newtown Massacre. I was jarred by that word. "Massacre" feels like something adults do to one another. And it seemed to move the event so quickly into the past, which felt so dangerous.

I went to the Web, where Wikipedia listed 220 "massacres" around the world in chronological order beginning in 61 CE. Yes Newtown, chillingly, had been added, already history. In the description of each massacre, there was a number ranging from five to three hundred thousand, often followed by the phrase "men, women, and children." The time-honored ranking struck hard: Newtown: twenty children and six women. It was as if some sovereign arbiter had grabbed us by the throat and screamed PAY ATTENTION!

Do we know how?

As I write, our state representatives are spending their holiday breaks in their own bubbles of their constituencies. I imagine the cards arriving at their doors:

Merry Christmas, please ban assault weapons now!
Merry Christmas, God bless you for upholding our Second
Amendment Rights!

I imagine invisible parentheses by each message saying: *If you will only do what* **I** *think, everything will be fine. It's* **them** *that's the problem.*

There was only one other massacre on the Wikipedia list that happened in Connecticut. In 1637 "400–700" "mostly women, children, and old men" of the Pequot tribe were torched to death inside their Mystic River fort by English colonists convinced that God was on their side. What hasn't changed in 375 years is the American taste for the drug of certainty.

The problem isn't guns; it's our Mental Health System... as if there's a simple, single fix for the demons our souls are heir to.

Yeah, they passed those laws in Australia after that terrible shooting, but it wouldn't work here... as we cave inward from our insistent exceptionalism.

The shooter was just plain evil... The depth and breadth of tragedy, the complexity of what may be required in its wake, seems to eat our brains for breakfast.

I am reminded of a story my father used to tell. As a naval communications officer in Nagasaki six months after the atom bomb, he was charged with showing bigwigs around the devastation. "Hmm," one general responded, "considerable personnel damage here."

Considerable damage to personnel in Newtown, whose faces—I fear—we cannot bear to hold in front of the national psyche long enough to honor them with meaningful action. It is not that I have no need for the palliation of pushing away woe. As an Easterner I am prone to insulating myself from the mass shootings in the West and

South. As a Manhattanite, I admit to relief at hearing that the latest violent crime has occurred in one of the other boroughs. Perhaps this is evolutionary self-preservation, but a terrible shame attends it.

I slept fitfully Christmas Eve, waking again and again to sorrow. At one point, on the cusp of consciousness, I saw my friend from Newtown carry the body of his son, limp as King Lear's Cordelia, into the deliberating chambers of Congress…

Howl, howl, howl! O, you are men of stones!
Had I your tongues and eyes, I'd use them so
That heaven's vaults should crack!

It is a new year. How will they use their tongues?

Kristin Westbrook

First Time

That day.
I went for a test
After the Mother's Day miscarriage.
It was routine.
In the waiting room I overheard the doctor speaking into his dictaphone.
"It's breast cancer," he said.

I thought wow that has to suck to hear those words.

I was there to have a procedure which would clear my fallopian tubes.

A test the nurse Said would increase my chances of getting pregnant by 75 percent

After the test.

"Have you had a mammogram recently?"

I need one.

We can do it now.

Three hours later,

He showed me the screen.

He was 99 percent sure.

I had breast cancer.

I thought wow is that what you say to all of your patients,

Dr. Doom and Gloom.

It looked like a monster on his screen.

Like a dark-gray sea creature with tendrils reaching out to strangle anything in sight

Then finally an electric shock.

Cracks of lighting strike.

I remember thinking about war

About soldiers and how they face death.

Was this going to be my personal war?

I've told this story a thousand times.

It never gets better in the telling of it.

It's always a lousy story.

I'm numb to it now.

I don't feel much looking back on that day.

My husband's favorite band is the Supersuckers.

This was a super sucker day.

I don't want to read it aloud or speak about it or have it in my mind.

It was the day all the color washed out of me.

My vision of the future floating down a dry dirt river.

My youth washed away with a single sentence from a stranger and a computer screen.

These memories need to be buried deep into the ground. To the center of the earth.

No one should ever dig them out.

If Picasso Was My Plastic Surgeon

Missing pieces, torn apart.
Deconstructed.
A profile.
Plump, open lips.
One tooth overlaps the other.
Large tears spill down the left side of the face,
Pouring out of green eyes.
Lashes burned away.
Heart flattened.
Body pulled apart.
Dissected.
Removed.
Cut up negative space.
Long crooked, blood red semi-circle line across the belly.
Navel new.
Borrowing from Peter to pay Paul.
Missing breast sculpted and reformed.
Scarred.
A thin circular line annotates the missing nipple like a proofreader's mark.
The torso looks like a smile and a wink.

A deep dark hole left where she used to be.
A funked-up tattered construction paper collage, colors faded.
Pictured in black and white.

Bob Wine

Beer versus Advice

It was a warm day on Spring Break vacation in Mexico, and our group of young lads found ourselves splashing in the ocean waves, with the most picaresque scene in the shadow of huge cliffs above us. As we swam, we could see the bottom of the ocean where there were rocks, some intimidatingly large peppered through underwater dunes of sand. What were the hidden mysteries of the deep? The beach was crowded and with a lot of jousting going on to obtain the best spot for access to the water. Added to this was the prospect of burning oneself to a crisp in the tropical sun. Having sharp elbows, which I developed in the New York subway, I was able to secure a great spot near the water. While I was prepared to have a wild time, it definitely got a little wilder than expected.

I watched some kids out in the water on surfboards. Even though the water looked calm, there was a strong, dangerous undertow. No one wants to get caught in that. I am a strong swimmer and was looking forward to going out far, the powerful waves did not worry me, but that may have been due to the libations we had along.

We were a bunch of school friends and we made sure to have lots of brewski. We were having a good time with no worry in the world— the beers made sure of that. We had tons of chips and cookies, a treat that makes for a young man's balanced meal with any beer. We were more than a little soused, and with the added sugar, the combination was not one that would lead to sensible decisions.

Some of my friends were good at surfing. It is very exciting to see them hop on the board, swim out to the wave, and ride it into the shore. Egos play a big part in the surfing game. Not being a surfer and not having the guts to do it in that moment, I chose to watch. However, when my friend egged me on to go out on a board, the peer pressure in combination with the beer, or should it be called "beer pressure," I thought, "Just go for it, what could happen?"

The easy part was to swim out on the board in a prone position, but standing on the board was quite challenging. After a few flops I was able to stand. And just as I did, a giant wave consumed me. Frightened, I sunk like a rock. So much for my beach and beer-headed hubris.

I did get a breath before the wave hit, but my confidence that I would survive was low with the strong undertow. It was rather precarious, and as I mentioned, I was a little "toasted." But in this most desperate of moments, and maybe by some miracle of luck, I recalled advice my father had given me.

"Roll yourself into a ball, and the wave will carry you to the shore."

Not always listening to my father, I chose to heed his advice. I held my breath and curled up like a ball. Nothing is more frightening than seeing a wave hover over you like a hungry beast and then come crashing down, devouring you in one swift bite. I thought it was all over, but in a ball, I bounced around not seeing the shore.

My father's advice worked! I finally felt the sand underneath me. After a few scrapes and a wounded ego, I made it to shore. Relieved, I thanked the ocean for taking me home, and my father for his wisdom. I can't remember when he told me the "roll into a ball" advice, but I am thankful it found its way to the surface of my submerged brain on that day. As for those friends, I never let them pressure me into anything ever again.

Marianne Wrobleski

CYCLONE

ANNA LEANED ON WILLIE, HER hand on his shoulder, while Willie stretched his arm wrapping it around Anna's waist. Silently, they both peered into the pool below Luna Park's welcoming tower. Hundreds had crowded together for the July 4th festivities at Coney Island, many lining up for a ride on the Cyclone, while others strolled on the boardwalk. Sunbathers filled the sandy beach, and those who were lucky enough to afford a ten-cent hot dog devoured them happily.

Next to Anna, a girl sung *The Man I Love* adoringly to her sweetheart, a song popular that summer of 1928. Mothers hovered over their excited children, and dogs ran slipshod up and down sun-bleached planks. The merriment in the air was as hot as that summer afternoon in Brooklyn. But Anna was elsewhere; she had something on her mind.

Willie could see that Anna was preoccupied. He guessed she may be waiting for a proposal or a commitment—he sensed she wanted something more than their infrequent dates. He remained quiet. Willie had something on his mind, too. So for now, he satisfied himself with the pretty picture that was Anna. He thought of playing with the curls hanging loosely under her French beret or of tightening his squeeze around her waist, or maybe just smoothing his hand over her silky flowered dress. How adorable she was—how fresh, how young, how inviting.

But soon their silence begged for interruption. Taking both her hands in his, Willie kissed Anna's cheek lightly, and speaking softly, asked, "What's going on with you, kid?" Anna made a face; she hated when he called her kid. She assumed that at twenty-two she was a full-grown woman. From the looks she got when she walked down the street, Anna knew she was a catch and she was smart enough to know Willie wasn't the only fish in the sea. Sure, she'd been coy with him; she loved playing the coquette. Willie had been fun, but something was about to change.

Anna found herself looking for words but not finding them. After struggling a bit, she turned to face him. She had to tell him today. She mouthed the sentence that could change both their lives: "Willie, I think I'm pregnant," but no sound came from her lips. Standing so close to him and saying nothing, she simply studied his face. It was a nice enough face. But now she noticed a mole-like mark on the side of his neck that she had overlooked before. She concentrated on a stringy grayish hair flying loose from the blemish. She then took a step back and took note of the ridiculous suspenders yanking up his absurdly high-waisted pants. Suddenly his twenty-eight years looked much older to her.

Anna thought of what she wanted. She knew if it weren't for the current situation, she'd go on dreaming her dreams, ones which she once believed could one day become real. She envisioned living in Paris; she had read that women could live independent lives there. She imagined being dressed in the fashions of Coco Chanel or writing poetry in her left bank garret or sipping martinis with Hemingway and the Fitzgeralds in one of many cafes in St. Germain or Montparnasse. She would be the heroine in one of Hemingway's novels, giving her the instant and lasting fame that she would never find in her small Brooklyn surroundings.

Willie nudged her out of her reverie. "Hey, let's go for a walk." "I've got a better idea," she replied, unexpectedly invigorated. "Let's go on the Cyclone." Anna knew Willie didn't care much for the ups and downs of roller coasters. But she also knew Willie would want to please her, so as she knew he would, he wandered off to buy the tickets. As they stood on line, looking up at the wooden monster, Anna became more and more elated. "What's this all about?" wondered Willie. Only moments ago, Anna had been demure, almost sullen. Now she was game to go on this crazy ride. "What is it with women; one moment they're one thing, another moment something else," mused Willie.

Waiting for the ride to come to a standstill, they watched as a little girl in a pink frilly dress burst into screaming tears after dropping her doll into a muddy puddle. Quick as lighting, Willie bent to retrieve the doll, drying it on his shirt and gently handing it to the child. "He's so good with kids, such a natural," thought Anna, gazing awkwardly at this tender scene.

The Cyclone came to a stop. Dazed riders lifted themselves out of their seats and stumbled unsteadily to the ground. Willie and Anna climbed on, fastening themselves into their seats as best they could. They held the safety bar tightly, their differing anticipations separating them for the moment. Then they were off. Up they climbed, the deafening clickety-clack sounds ricocheting off the tracks. Reaching the summit, Anna looked down, holding her breath as she took in the decline. Willie, full of dread, closed his eyes. Then down again, faster than light; it all happened so quickly. Then another upturn, then a twisting downward plunge. Anna screamed with delight; Willie held on for dear life.

Moments later, Anna's heady excitement was interrupted by a feeling that something within her body had shifted. She felt pain, then a surge…a flow of something moving within then without her. She felt a hot liquid between her legs and sensed a growing stain forming on the flower field of her dress. She was not alarmed.

Next to her, Willie seemed to have conquered his anxiety and was now loving the thrashing speed of the ride. Something, more than anxiety, had lifted for him. Glancing at Anna, he realized what was clear to him, and screaming into the wind he shouted, "Anna, I love you. I love you." At the same time, Anna, her own voice jubilant, was shouting, "I'm free, I'm free." Neither could hear the other's exclamations over the roar of the ride.

The Cyclone screeched to a stop and holding onto one another, Anna and Willie swaggered away laughing, both, for the moment, liberated from the day's earlier ruminations. Anna's pain had ceased; she only felt relief. Willie hadn't noticed the spot growing on Anna's dress. She asked for his jacket feigning a chill. The length of the jacket would cover her stain of freedom.

The Coney Island sun was beginning to slide away, streaking the sky with deep pink hues. A half-moon was rising. As they walked,

Anna was thinking of her life…what adventures awaited her. She was her young dreamer self again. Willie, with the realization of his love for Anna that only moments ago he had surrendered into the air but not yet to her, had grown sullen. He was once again Willie, that man who wasn't so sure of himself. With heavy heart, he knew he had to tell her today. But how would he express his love for Anna and at the same time tell her he had a wife and two kids.

Conversation with My Brain

Brain, brain, go away, come again another day…brain, brain, go away, come again another day…

The slightly altered childhood nursery rhyme that I now hummed to lull me to sleep wasn't working. Nor was counting sheep.

Oh, brain, you little demon, why must you keep torturing me? Don't you know I have to sleep? Why do you keep going on and on, interrupting my drowsiness with your relentless chatter? Who asked you, anyway? What a nuisance you've become! I know; I know. I said I *know* already. Yes, you're right—I shouldn't have gotten so angry today about Aunt Betty's call. But, dear brain, please forget what I said. File that episode somewhere in that fat organ of yours. Let it go! I apologized! It's over! Oh, so you don't think my apology was genuine. Brain, let me ask you something, have you ever had to spend hours on the phone with Aunt Betty while she complains about the injustices she suffers at the hands of the nursing home staff—how they let her sit for hours without so much as a smile or hello; how Nurse Lucy purposely ties the blood pressure cuff so tight that it leaves her bruised; or how the Jello is not hard or soft enough or too green and what dyes are they putting in that shit anyway?! And did *you* ever have to listen to her bursts of anger about how Uncle Stan loved his mother more than he loved her? Oh, you have. OK, well then, try to understand why I get so frustrated with Aunt Betty and let the whole thing go. Oh, so now you're telling me you *did* let it go and it's me who's hanging on to things.

Oh, brain, sometimes I wish I didn't have you lolling about in my head all the time. Truly, I don't wish you any harm. I just want to be able to turn you off when I want to shut down. Why don't you come with a switch, or better yet, a remote control? The truth is you're probably as sick of me as I am of you. And to be fair, I do appreciate you, really I do. You've served me well all these years, but what's this latest trick of yours that won't allow me to sleep? What's in it for you? You say you're trying to help me, but it's become a constant tug of war! Are you really two brains—the good one and the bad one? Why suggest before bedtime that I meditate and drink warm milk to help me sleep when you just turn around and bring up Aunt Betty? You're a bit schizoid. Why not just let me concentrate on one thing at a time rather than fire me up with all your manic rubbish!

Oh, brain, you're driving me crazy. Who the hell do you think you are? And people call me a control freak. Ha! They should meet the likes of you. Are we going to be able to coexist, you and I? We'd better give some serious thought to our separation. I'm really fed up!

FAREWELL

Sandy died. Her son had called Rob that morning; Rob called Greg, who told Cloe, who called me. "She won't suffer anymore," Cloe had said. "She was such a nice person."

My heart quickened and then stopped for a moment while a single tear burned its way down my cheek. I closed my eyes trying to find a way to what I was feeling. Why is it that one can see and think more clearly, more profoundly with closed eyes? Pictures began to form, one after another. I saw Sandy on the beach we so loved, far from

Manhattan, close to the lighthouse on Fire Island. I could almost taste the salty air, feel the sand scraping the insides of my toes, hear the waves approaching then crashing followed by a swooshing sound as each wave slid onto the shoreline and quickly evaporated into the sand. That beach was our favorite place to be. We'd go there in winter, fall, spring, and summer, no matter what the weather.

In spring, we'd walk in fog so thick until we became blurry images, unrecognizable to the day and to each other. We became sea ghosts, wayfaring pirates searching for treasure and gold coins in the sand. In summer, we'd feign late-afternoon illnesses to get away from work and on to the highway heading out to sea before rush-hour traffic thwarted our getaway. I smiled at all the happy seaside hours we spent together and now hoped Sandy would be returned to the ocean as a mermaid or sea nymph or some translucent mystical fish, swimming out to sea to happier times.

My eyes opened, searching for solace, and fell upon an image of a Monet painting of water lilies sketched across my desk calendar. Admiring this scene, I wondered what Monet may have been thinking as he painted each delicate pink petal. Was he even thinking about water lilies? So many times I've lost myself in his garden landscapes that seem to reach way beyond the frame. His clouds moved; his suns brightened my world. I remembered the time I visited Giverny, thrilled to finally see this expansive space of exploding color. At first, I was stunned at the smallness of the gardens—beautiful, yes, but beauty in a tiny universe and not the grand world of flora and sky of my imagination. The Japanese-style bridge that had seemed to expand from one end of the world to another could probably be traversed in a dozen or so steps. So odd and surprising are our perceptions and so often how utterly wrong.

Returning my eyes to the crowded maze of papers on my desk, I rustled through them, looking for the photos of Sandy I had recently found—Sandy on the beach tossing grapes to the seagulls, Sandy leaning on a lifeguard chair, brushing the sand from her hair, her gray Duke sweatshirt wrapping her against the salty wind. There she was in Grenada, her fair but slightly sunburned cheeks glowing brighter and brighter as the sun dipped deeper into the horizon. I felt such sadness knowing that she had not been able to see her beloved ocean once more.

These thoughts of times past that were once so happy now seemed so bittersweet. The memories would always be there, but my friend had gone away. Looking at the photos once more, I whispered, "Good-bye sweet Sandy. I will miss you," and then placed them face-down on my desk, turned off the desk lamp, and went to bed.

BIOGRAPHIES OF THE WRITERS

ALLEN DICKSTEIN WAS A HOSPITAL administrator and worked in diverse areas of care including Oncology, Family Medicine, and Pediatrics. In a previous life, Allen was a joyful yoga teacher and had the pleasure of having many wonderful students. During the 1970s and 1980s, he sported a thick head of ringlet curls with a dark mustache. Presently, his head of curls is a short haircut, and he has a salt-and-pepper beard. He is an avid attendee at his local gym and a walker in Central Park. He began writing essays after joining a cancer care writing group, which proved to be a wonderful healing process.

Isaac Dmitrovsky is a professional software developer, an amateur investor, and an aspiring writer. He was born and raised in New York City and still lives there. This paragraph marks the first time he has referred to himself in the third person.

Judith Elaine Halek, Director of Birth Balance, lives in NYC with her devoted Calico companion LuLu. After almost three decades of assisting over 2500 babies come into the world, Judith was diagnosed with Stage III lymphoma on August 19, 2014. Writing has been her most "potent medicine" and jumped-started a memoir in the making, documenting her transition from *Birth Maven to Cancer Thriver*.

Jacqueline Ruth Johnson is a registered nurse at Mount Sinai Beth Israel Petrie Campus in the oncology unit. Cancer became an unwelcomed visitor when her mother was diagnosed with metastatic breast cancer in 1979 and left this life in 1984. In 2010, Jacqueline was diagnosed with endometrial cancer. A zest for life was reawakened through the determination to overcome cancer and to bring awareness to all women, in particular, women of color, about gynecological cancers. Motivated by The Write Treatment Writing Workshop, she returned to school for her master's in nursing. Jacqueline is a member of the local Toastmasters and was invited to be an ambassador for the American Cancer Society New York City region. She participates in the Narrative Medicine Writing Workshop for caregivers at Gilda's Club. The love of a supportive family encourages her daily.

Melody Johnson relocated to Austin, Texas, after many years in New York City. A two-time survivor of breast cancer, she joined The Write Treatment Workshops in late 2011. Her poetry has been published in annual issues of *Oberon* as well as *The Acorn, Pifonoca, Women's Voices*, and *The Fayetteville Times*. When not writing poetry, she is working on "Camp Casey Songs," a collection of short stories based on her memories of Busan, South Korea.

Cristina Liann has been a member of Roosevelt Writing Workshop for some time, while recuperating from cancer treatment. Primarily a poet, writing at Roosevelt opened her up to the genres of memoir and short story. She has been a past participant in the downtown poetry scene reading at Cornelia St. Café, Nightingale Lounge, and poetry fests. She is currently working on poetry submissions and putting together a chapbook. Cristina has a BA in English Literature and Creative Writing. Besides writing and reading widely, Cristina is active in her community and tries to travel as often as possible.

Peggy Liegel was diagnosed with stage III breast cancer in the winter of 2007. She is still in treatment (hormonal) at Mount Sinai Beth Israel Hospital, New York City. It was Peggy's good fortune to be a writer in Emily Rubin's beginning workshops there. The Write Treatment process was transformative and healing. Peggy continues her self-journey—yearly growing a new tree ring and branches for singing birds by sinking deeper roots on a solid, safer, richer ground. She walks in "currently land" of expanding new normals, creating fifty-two day journeys with calendar in hand (seven a year), experiencing morning, noon, and night shifting. She is also a long-distance Reiki practitioner who believes in the power of love and finding peace inside oneself. Peggy admires greatly feats of balance: yours, mine, ours.

Susan Massad I am a voracious reader, but writing had never been fun. It was always a task to be done—an obligatory letter to parents and grands, a term paper, a professional article or talk, and then came emails. Retirement from fifty plus years of medical practice and, shortly following this, a recurrence of breast cancer slowed me down. A time to reassess, and concentrate on what did I want to do today? I discovered writing—plays, memoirs, stories, and an occasional rhyme—always done with others, writing and reading together, sharing and appreciating. It has been a wonderful gift in my midseventies to discover this new passion. Writing with the Writer Treatment Writing Workshops has been a source of inspiration and great joy.

Michelle McCartney... Hallo there. Michelle here, and I write from Ireland. I found Emily a long time ago on the Internet in a report on her project. I asked to join and she said *YES*. Between the group, Emily and Caroline M. Sun (now sadly deceased but very much loved) I feel connected and cherished, not just as a writer or as a cancer vixen but as a person. Bless you all. It has been such fun...and there's more!

Jack Robert Nix. In fall 2007, I learned I had cancer. As a way of making sense of it, I have tried to put the feelings and fears and hopes into words I call poetry. It is a way to bypass the tedium of "why me" with all its attendant wallowing and creatively engage cancer. And live life. The weekly writing workshops run by Emily Rubin have provided a wonderful way to channel that creative energy.

Juan Pagan. Born, raised, and still living on the Lower East Side... my parents migrated from Puerto Rico and met here on the Lower East Side. I am a single father, raising my daughter...into my third year fighting cancer....

Connie Perry is an artist, a comic performer, publicist, and writer. She joined the late Sue Ribner's Writing Workshop at Roosevelt Hospital in early 2014, just after her cancer treatment—her "hysterical-ectomy." She currently writes with Emily Rubin's Write Treatment Workshops. As a freelance book publicist, Connie connects authors to media. As a theatre usher, she frequently needs to diffuse customer service stress by performing her one-woman show *Theatre Obsession: Saucy Tales from the Aisle.* Also, a visual arts project utilizing unique DeaR postcards is blossoming at instagram.com/dearcards.

Isaac Read. When I was a student, history events were recorded as BC (Before Christ) and AD (Anno Domini—In the year of the Lord). I am writing a personal history, BC (Before Cancer) and AC (After Cancer). The first part, BC, is not that good. The second part, AC, looks great!

Susan Ribner (May 4, 1940–Oct 14, 2014) coauthored two nonfiction young adult books: *The Martial Arts* (Harper & Row), with Richard Chin, and *Right On! An Anthology of Black Literature*, under the pseudonym Rebecca Moon, coedited with Bradford Chambers (New American Library). She published numerous articles on women's history, children's literature, and the martial arts. A selection from her memoir, *Sister Stories*, "Front Lawn/Back Yard Stories," was awarded First Place in the Writers@Work 2011 Memoir Contest and was published in *Quarterly West* (Issue 72). For twenty-one years, Ribner taught writing workshops at Hunter College (CUNY). In addition, she taught memoir workshops sponsored by Poets and Writers, was a tutor training in seminars at Bank Street College of Education, and led a creative writing workshop for cancer patients at St. Luke's Hospital in New York City. With colleague Ron Grant, she created the Gribner Nonfiction Manuscript Workshops, which were held in the United States in 2005 and in the Prague Summer Writing Program from 2006–2010. Recipient of a Jerome Foundation Fellowship for a residency at the Anderson Center for Interdisciplinary Studies, Ms. Ribner received an MFA in Creative Nonfiction from the University of New Orleans/Prague Summer Seminars (2004), an MA in TESOL from Hunter College, and an MA in Comparative Government (Cornell University). Susan continued writing until her death from complications of ovarian cancer in 2014.

Joanne Rogovin has thirty-five years of experience in leadership, change management, strategic planning, communications strategies and plans, and designing organizations so that they are most effective. She has been a volunteer group leader for sixteen years at Gay Men's Health Crisis, providing therapy and group facilitation for people with HIV/AIDS. She currently volunteers at the Arts & Business Council as an executive coach to the artistic director. She holds BA and MA degrees from Boston University and an MSW from Yeshiva University, and she is a licensed clinical social worker in New York State.

Eve Roshevsky As a book editor at Doubleday, Eve worked with Nobel Prize winner Isaac Bashevis Singer on his multi-volume memoir *Love & Exile* and with a number scholars writing commentaries for the Anchor Bible. As a staff executive for Women of Reform Judaism, she coordinated projects for their six hundred sisterhoods and edited a collection of spiritual writings, *Covenant of the Heart.* Eve studied voice and piano at Oberlin and Juilliard, and still plays piano after fifty years, most recently Bach, Blues, and Ragtime. She did volunteer work in Israel from 1968 to 1969 and speaks fluent Hebrew. She recently moved to the green North Country of upstate New York from Manhattan, after living there for forty years, the last eight of them with her feline roommate, and muse, Brillo.

Lara Stein is a writer in New York City who lives happily with her husband and son, and right breast. Lest you think her left breast disappeared into Dr. Seuss's Kaverns of Krock, it simply reinvented itself as a nimble-footed creature jumping high on a trampoline in her young son's imagination. In real life, Lara goes by another name, but everything else in her bio is true, including the trampoline and the lucky plastic prize horse from that day at the Jersey Shore.

Caroline Marie Sun (July 20, 1962–December 9, 2014) was born in Ashland, Wisconsin, on July 20, 1962. She passed away from the complications of colon-rectal cancer at home, in Fresh Meadows, Queens, New York, on December 9, 2014. She was a graduate of the Bronx High School of Science. Originally destined to become a physician, Caroline changed course and attended the University of Pennsylvania School of Law. She worked at the internationally acclaimed law firm of Fish & Neave specializing in patents and trademarks and intellectual property. She also taught as a professor at Queens College, the City University of New York, after earning a master's degree in

English Literature from Hunter College. After enjoying much profes-
sional success as a lawyer, Caroline returned to her first love, being a
visual artist. Caroline wrote this of herself: "I paint the Secret Lives of
Animals. I look for the emotion between animals and ourselves. My
work has a narrative quality and there are stories, sometimes factual,
sometimes fictional, behind each piece."

Belinda Ward

Born in a county with the motto "The rose, emblem of harmony"
in…England that most green and pleasant land.

Likes throwing pots, dogs, magazines, fish&chips, the seaside, grow-
ing herbs, French chemists.

In pondering writing, I love the freedom of a blank piece of paper.
You can start anywhere.

Never a dull moment, every day is a new and beautiful experience
(when I want to stay in bed) favourite sayings

Daughter, sister, wife. The love and laughter of family and friends is
the most precious thing.

Always asking "what's next?"

Eloïse Watt spent four decades acting, teaching, and writing in New
York and now lives in Maine.

Kristin Smith Westbrook had the opportunity to begin working
professionally during her studies at The School of Visual Arts in

1988. Since then, she has enjoyed a career in graphic design as an art director and creative director for over twenty years. She has worked for national publications including *Elle and House Beautiful*, as well as *Sears* and *DIRECTV*. Her experience extends to many other creative fields such as residential mural painting, woodworking, stage design, set construction, acting, sewing, and retail display. Her other interests include English-style horseback riding, Bikram yoga, cycling, and home decoration. She is currently exploring writing as a means of expressing her experience with breast cancer. She is grateful to Emily Rubin and all the members of The Write Treatment Writing Workshops for their support and their wonderful stories.

Bob Wine was born in Brooklyn, but he grew up in Bronx and earned a BS degree in Mathematics at City College. Bob worked in the computer industry for more than fifty years, including development on the Ticketron, Off-track Betting, the Jersey lottery systems. He facilitated support groups for neuromuscular diseases at NYU Medical Center. Since retiring he has been concentrating on wildlife, cityscape, and sports photography. He studied with photographers David Muench and Jay Maisel. Bob plays the Shakuhachi flute, a traditional Japanese bamboo instrument. He has performed in Japan and at the Cherry Blossom Festival at the Brooklyn Botanic Gardens and other locations. Photographs on view at www.BobWinePhotography.com and www.Bndwine.com.

Marianne Wrobleski is a phantom having been relegated to Mother Earth some decades ago. She gets lost in the spring and finds it difficult to meet deadlines. In the winter, she is so much of a recluse that the Carthusian order of cloistered nuns in the south of France have invited her to next year's three-month silent retreat. Her stories are formed from remembered adventures of her very afflicted mind.

Having heard about the Roosevelt and Beth Israel writing workshops after being diagnosed with cancer and while still working in the field of cancer clinical trials, she wanted nothing more to do with cancer. However, one afternoon spent among this group of talented and compassionate writers made her reconsider. What visions and revelations exploded onto a page in that two-hour session! The classes led by Emily Rubin are a saving grace for many and the best medicine any doctor could prescribe.

EMILY RUBIN, EDITOR/INSTRUCTOR

EMILY RUBIN IS AN AUTHOR and writing instructor. She has run the Write Treatment Workshops since 2011 and has been a breast cancer survivor herself since 2010. She is the author of Stalina, a winner of the Amazon Debut Novel Award, and a recipient of the Sarah Verdone Writers Award. You can find more at www. emilyrubin.net.

Lauren Flick has an almost twenty-year career in television and film. A storyteller at heart, she has worked with major networks, including NBC, CBS, CNBC, and AMC. After losing her father to pancreatic cancer in 2008, she was drawn to the Write Treatment Workshops.

LAUREN IS A STORYTELLER WHO has worked in television and film for almost twenty years. She has worked for such notable networks as NBC, CBS, CNBC, and AMC. Lauren was drawn to this project because, as most of us, cancer touched her life in 2008, when she lost her father to pancreatic cancer. She has been inspired by this writing program, through the stories featured in the anthology but mostly by the voice it has given to those who often feel unheard during such challenging times.